BROKEN BY LOVE

The Story of an Atheist Turned Pastor

by
Cris Cazarine

Watersprings
PUBLISHING

Broken by Love: The Story of an Atheist Turned Pastor
Published by Watersprings Publishing,
a division of Watersprings Media House, LLC.
P.O. Box 1284 Olive Branch, MS 38654
www.waterspringspublishing.com
Contact the publisher for bulk orders and permission requests.

Copyright © 2024 Cris Cazarine. All rights reserved.

No part of this publication may be reproduced, distributed, or transmitted in any form or by any means, including photocopying, recording, or other electronic or mechanical methods, without the prior written permission of the publisher, except in the case of brief quotations embodied in critical reviews and certain other noncommercial uses permitted by copyright law.

Editorial team: Paula Macena and Latoyia Williams

Printed in the United States of America.

ISBN-13: 979-8-9894494-6-0

Table of Contents

CHAPTER 1   Towering Tree Escape. 1

CHAPTER 2   Let the Games Begin 4

CHAPTER 3   My Own ROM-COM. 9

CHAPTER 4   Worse than the Birds and the Bees Talk. 14

CHAPTER 5   Church Retreat From Hell 17

CHAPTER 6   Time to Run Away 24

CHAPTER 7   Betrayed by the One Closest to Me. 33

CHAPTER 8   This Time Has to Work 36

CHAPTER 9   The Other Side of the Story 41

CHAPTER 10   Things Will Be Different Now. 47

CHAPTER 11   I was Out of Control. 53

CHAPTER 12   Strange Religious Beliefs 56

CHAPTER 13   And Keep on Spiraling Out of Control. 63

CHAPTER 14   How Things Got so Bad. 71

CHAPTER 15   Back to Where it All Started 79

CHAPTER 16   Another Weekend Alone, Another Party 82

CHAPTER 17   Me Too 86

CHAPTER 18   Not the ROM-COM Happy Ending I Wished For. 93

CHAPTER 19   Is He the One?. 100

CHAPTER 20   The Oktoberfest Affair 109

CHAPTER 21   Meet the Parents 112

CHAPTER 22   Not Even the Ghosts Liked Me. 118

iv   Broken by Love: The Story of an Atheist Turned Pastor

CHAPTER 23   The Stars Spoke 120

CHAPTER 24   The Stepmom's Predictions 127

CHAPTER 25   She Felt Completely, Utterly Defeated 132

CHAPTER 26   A Strange Invitation and a New Family 136

CHAPTER 27   Players Will Play 140

CHAPTER 28   I Have a Baby 144

CHAPTER 29   Reality Started to Set In 147

CHAPTER 30   Moving to the US 151

CHAPTER 31   Back to Brazil 155

CHAPTER 32   Back to the US 158

CHAPTER 33   She is Just a Friend 160

CHAPTER 34   The Red Flags Were All Over the Place 167

CHAPTER 35   The Cycle Started all Over Again 170

CHAPTER 36   Wasn't She Just a Friend? 174

CHAPTER 37   The End of a Romantic, the Birth of an Atheist 177

CHAPTER 38   It is Time to Have Fun! 181

CHAPTER 39   That is How we Met 185

CHAPTER 40   The Pot and the Kettle 191

CHAPTER 41   Friday Night Hangouts 196

CHAPTER 42   I Was Forced into a Bible Study 198

CHAPTER 43   Beach, Beer, and Bible 203

CHAPTER 44   The Epiphany 206

CHAPTER 45   The Proposal 213

CHAPTER 46   Changes Started Happening 217

CHAPTER 47   The Wedding 219

Happily, Ever After 222

About the Author 225

CHAPTER 1

Towering Tree Escape

Memories of my first childhood home came back in dreams I never quite remembered when I woke. But whenever I visited São Paulo, there was some part of me that subconsciously remembered, that still felt claustrophobic in that big city. There were just buildings and buildings, and nothing else was in sight. Olímpia was both crueler and kinder to me, in a way.

It was a small town by Brazilian standards, safer for a kid my age. In Praça Da Matriz, the town square, stood the Igreja Matriz, a Catholic church with a bell tower that seemed to stretch for miles in my young eyes. I'd walk there barefoot, my feet slapping against the concrete streets. There was space to run and room to play with the handful of neighborhood kids I'd spend time with while Mom and Dad were away. Anyone with a typical childhood would most likely have nice memories of Olímpia, despite the tourist trap it's now become decades later. It should have been a good place to grow up. But all I took from my time there was the ability to pinpoint where everything began to go wrong.

I didn't know what was happening with my parents until about a year later when Madonna, my stepmom, came into the picture and began filling in the blanks for me. Mom had already been gone for a while. I didn't know where she went;

Dad wouldn't speak about it, and all Grandma said was that she had left and wasn't coming back. "She dropped you off to go get some baby bottles," she told me once. "She never came back. I don't know if she ever will."

I didn't know enough to question it much. It was just the way it was—Mom was here, and now she wasn't. We weren't allowed to go wherever she was and didn't know enough to want to anyway. Looking back, I know it was all traumatizing—of course it was—but as a kid, you don't think about these things. You don't wonder why you and your siblings were sent to live with your Grandma and shipped off with your uncle in São Paulo for two months; you just go. You don't question the bruises on your Mom's neck that you accidentally saw nearly two years ago, that you weren't even sure you saw at all.

Mom would come by once a month now, only on Sundays, and only from eight in the morning to six in the evening—never, ever more than that—to whisk away my brother, sister, and me and spend the day with her. In Madonna's eyes, it was more than Mom deserved.

Madonna and I would meticulously wax the tiled, red front porch together. To Madonna, cleanliness was next to godliness. It was up to the women of the house, excluding my youngest sister for the time being, to ensure it held up to her standard.

"You know," she'd tell me as we waxed, my fingers cramping. "Just because someone's a biological mother doesn't make them a mom. A *real* mom is the one who raises you. A real mom *stays*." She shrugged as if it were nothing more than an afterthought. "Just saying. You're luckier than you realize."

I knew what she meant—that she was a good person, while my mother was a bad one. But I wouldn't say anything back; just kept waxing the floor until it shone, red and non-sticky, with a close enough resemblance to blood. As soon as Madonna would tell me I'd done enough for the day, I'd run to the towering tree in our front yard and latch onto it, quickly climbing to my favorite branch. The tree loomed above me, and it felt like another world. Maybe that was why I loved it so much, why I developed an attachment to it—it felt far away enough from everything, from those bloody tiles and my stepmother's sour expression, that they didn't feel like they mattered anymore. I'd lean my head against the trunk and imagine I could feel it breathing, living. Everything was so small in comparison to this tree. I was so small.

CHAPTER 2

Let the Games Begin

"How are you holding up? You're so strong. I'm here for you."

The sympathy in the woman's nasally voice was sickening. I scowled, keeping my head down as I scarfed down my sandwich so Dad wouldn't notice. I glanced at my younger siblings, who both happily munched on their fries, clueless as to what was wrong with what was happening in front of us: Dad, sitting with his back straight, the pure essence of confidence and superiority—and a variety of women all around him, leaning toward him, all itching to touch him. It was a regular occurrence and had been for months. Today, I counted eight of them.

Despite this being a somewhat regular occurrence, I found it gross every time. I was both fascinated and repulsed by how much attention he got. The one closest to him that day was the youngest at the table, sitting so close to my Dad that she was practically on his lap. I didn't know her name, and I didn't particularly want to. Besides, what all these women didn't know was that he already had his eye on his secretary, Madonna. They could coo over him all they wanted; in the end, Madonna was the last one standing. She won.

As their relationship developed, before she moved in, I began to find bits and pieces of her all over the house. Some of her hair in the shower, her flip-flops by the door, the smell of her food wafting from the kitchen into the living room, filling the house with its steam (this was one of the few bonuses of having Madonna around—Mom had never been much of a cook). But my least favorite thing to find was the notes.

Carefully stacked on my Mom's vanity, which she'd left behind at my Dad's house, a pile of sticky notes written in my father's and Madonna's handwriting, all of them addressed to each other. Exchange after exchange, back and forth. Jealousy rose in my throat like bile. I almost felt betrayed. But still, I read through them, one by one; the more I read, the angrier I felt myself become. How dare she come into our lives so easily? It felt like it took her no effort at all—one day, Mom was here, and the next, it was Madonna, always here, always with something to say, taking all of the love and attention from Dad that should've been reserved for me and my siblings. Up until she came around, I still felt that love from him, even with the things he'd say to us sometimes. But with her arrival, any semblance of paternal affection was gone.

Shaking with envy, I ripped up all of the notes and flushed them down the toilet. *There*, I thought. *How does it feel to have love taken from you, too?* I wasn't living with Dad then, so I quickly rushed home to Grandma's right after. I knew Madonna would try to confront me eventually, so I bid my time the next few days, avoiding visiting Dad again. I tidied up my room three, four, five times. I swept the whole house. I always volunteered to wash the dishes. But I could only stay away for so long.

When I visited Dad's again, she was there, of course. I could feel her eyes on me the whole time, from the moment I walked through the door. I avoided her gaze as much as I could, but I couldn't get away from her for long. Eventually, while I was sweeping the floors alone, she cornered me.

"Cristiane, have you seen some letters?" Madonna asked. "From your father to me?"

I swallowed. I hated how she called them *letters*. It felt more important than *notes*. I kept sweeping, staring down at the floor. I was terrified, but I couldn't let her see that. I shook my head. "No," I said, trying to stop the tremor in my voice. "No. Where did you leave them?"

I could feel her scrutinizing me. When she didn't say anything, I finally looked up. Her eyes were boring into mine. "They were next to...your Dad's bed," she said with forced calm, a hidden threat in her voice. It was my *Mom's* bed, but I knew she'd never say that. She hated admitting that anything here ever belonged to my mother. She'd choose her words surgically, with the utmost precision. "Are you sure you haven't seen them?"

I shook my head again and looked back to the floor. It was the first time I ever told an outright lie. My face felt hot, and I couldn't shake the feeling that she could see right through me.

"*Cristiane*, I *know* you took them," she said, her voice harsher now, confirming my fears. "Give them to me."

"I don't have them," I insisted, trying to stay firm. What else could I do? Tell her they were in the sewers by now?

"Then *where are they?*"

"I don't *know*. I never saw them."

In one swift movement, she grabbed the broom from my hands and threw it on the floor. I flinched and jumped back. I still didn't look at her.

Without saying another word, she turned and left the room. I stood there, my heart pounding, trying to catch my breath. And then I picked up the broom and kept sweeping.

She kept me up, especially late that night. Madonna had this game she loved, which I called a shame game, but she most likely considered it as therapy for me. She'd sit me down in the living room late at night, alone, while the rest of the house was asleep, and begin her brainwashing routine.

This time, to start off, she handed me a piece of paper and colored pencils. "Draw a girl and a boy," she told me. And I, desperate for her approval, was happy to oblige.

I felt special, but I tried to swallow the feeling. I couldn't let her see how much I wanted to please her; my wanting felt childlike, and even though I was only eight years old, I hated feeling like a child. Madonna was double my age, and that fact felt like it meant something—like I was only half of her, and I needed to make up for the parts that I couldn't yet fulfill.

Before settling down and moving in with my Dad, she had dreams of going to college and becoming a psychologist. She constantly reminded me of how great of a person she was, a hero, to give up her dreams to raise my siblings and me. A teenager raising three kids that were not hers! How courageous, practically Herculean! Every time we'd go visit my mother, she'd scoff at us. "Not even a dog abandons her kids," she'd say. "But your Mom abandoned you." Looking back, I know she only wanted to make Mom look bad, so we'd stop visiting her. It worked. I didn't visit Mom for four years, but not only because I thought she was a bad person; I also began to believe that I wasn't worth staying for, and that's why Mom left. But Madonna stayed, so maybe I really was luckier than I realized. Right?

I don't remember what my drawing looked like, but I remember that I put everything I had into it. I used every colored pencil I had, down to the nub; I squinted and scrutinized all the little details, erased and redrew the hands again and again; I made sure to use Madonna's favorite colors for their clothes. When I finally finished, I handed it to her, a nervous wreck. She examined my drawing while I examined her, but no emotion slipped through the cracks on her face. She just held it and stared, and stared, and stared.

Finally, she looked at me. "Do you know what this drawing means?" she said. "It means you're a person who's extremely immature for your age." My heart sank. I wanted her to see me as an equal so badly. I was sick of being a child.

She went on to explain to me that she read in one of her many psychology books about the significance of kids' drawings and how they can say a lot about a child. Since she didn't go to college for psychology like she wanted, she tried to teach herself and would practice on me during nights like this. She called it her "great mission"; that God didn't let her go to college so she could use her talent for my betterment. Again, lucky me. So, we'd stay awake until what felt like 1 in the morning sometimes, talking about how terrible my Mom was and what I had to do to make sure I didn't follow in her footsteps. If I didn't do exactly what she said, I was bound to be a failure. And I couldn't say no—it would be ungrateful. When she was with the rest of the family, I'd hear her talking to them about me: "I think I'm getting through to her. She hasn't visited their Mom lately. Goodness, I'm doing such a good thing. I'm so proud of myself for being such a gift to her." She'd brag about herself to anyone who would listen.

The truth that I now know is that it was never a mission; it was an obsession. From what Madonna told me about her own childhood—consisting of an abusive and absent father, constantly living with violence—her life was always out of control. Although my family wasn't even close to well off, she saw my Dad as the pinnacle of financial stability, probably thanks to the convertible Volkswagen Puma he drove. Really, he was just a salesman picking up odd jobs, trying to make ends meet. But after the violent life she'd led, she deluded herself into believing she could find stability with my family, with my life. A part of me knew she was just a victim all along, the same as me. She only knew violence, and so she brought it along with her.

CHAPTER 3

My Own ROM-COM

My little brother stood in the doorway of what we called the girls' room. Our house was always full of people—our immediate family, plus maids, plus some of Madonna's family every now and then. There wasn't enough space for everyone, so the girls' room was where all of the younger girls of the house slept, including me, my little sister, and whatever other females were currently around.

I had just changed out of my pajamas to go play outside with my brother and the other neighborhood kids. Our sister was too young to play with us, so it was just my brother and I and a handful of random kids on our block. We were about eight years old by then and had been playing with them since we were six. I was rummaging under my bed, looking through my diaries; I'd just finished another one the night before and was trying to find a blank journal I could use.

I looked up, noticing him for the first time, and realized he now knew my secret hiding spot. "What are you doing here?!" I exclaimed, infuriated. "This is the *girls'* room!"

I stood up and went to slam the door, but my brother held it open. "Doesn't matter if it's the girls' room!" he said. "Dad said I can do whatever I want whenever I want because I'm a *man*. You're just a *girl*."

9

I rolled my eyes. I was used to Dad's and Madonna's patriarchal spiels, and now it seemed that they were finally getting to my brother's head. I went back to my bed and shoved my journals back under the bed. "Whatever," I said as I walked out the door, expecting him to follow. "Just don't tell Madonna about that, okay?"

"What, your stupid diaries?" he scoffed. "I don't *care*."

"Okay. Sure." I didn't believe him, but there also wasn't anything else I could do. "Let's just go."

As we walked outside, we were immediately greeted by the screams of other children running through the street, some on bikes, some barefoot, others rolling around in the grass. My eyes scanned them all quickly, searching for the one I really cared about. When I finally spotted him, his eyes were already on me-Massimo.

I happily skipped over to his spot on the street. His hands were dusty with chalk and drawn around him on the concrete was a life-size house. Or at least, as life-size as we could manage. We'd often draw each individual room, complete with kitchens and bedrooms and dining rooms, to playhouse with each other. It was everyone's favorite game. And no matter what anyone said, Massimo and I would always insist on being the parents.

Honestly, I'd liked him since I met him. He was sunkissed and beautiful and always had a smile for me. When my parents went to court for their divorce, and the other kids started looking at me differently, Massimo stayed the same. He was a great husband and father when we played house. As my home life worsened, this game became an escape for me. I could be a better wife and mother than Madonna, and my Mom could ever imagine being. And Massimo was my perfect partner.

Everyone knew that we liked each other—it was obvious. And yet, neither of us ever said a word to each other about it.

The closest I'd gotten to a confession was when Massimo graffitied a huge heart with our initials in it on the brick wall that surrounded my house. *M + C FOREVER* inside a heart-shaped drawing. I smiled for weeks after I saw it. I never asked him about it; I didn't need to. I was happy with things the way they were.

I knew that Madonna and my Dad would kill me if they ever found out about my crush, so I always prayed that my brother would keep it secret. *Please,* I thought to myself. *I have nothing else. Just let me have this.*

"Hi, honey," Massimo said, already in character. "How was work today?"

I blushed. It was easy to pretend that maybe, in some other universe, this was my reality: a big house that's never overcrowded, with a loving husband and a good job. A place where there is no girls' or boys' room, and men actually *can't* do whatever they want. In that universe, maybe I'm finally okay.

I was always a romantic at heart. I think I was born one. I think that when God first thought of me, He poured in me so much desire for love that could fit into a person but didn't save any for the people around me. There weren't many examples of great romances in my life, but I still found myself craving one, believing it was out there if I looked for it hard enough.

Since watching TV was my escape, I always found myself drawn to the romances. When Madonna wasn't busying me with cleaning or one of her infamous talks, I'd plop myself down in the living room on the sofa closest to the television to get the best view possible and watch for hours on end. Nothing could get to me when I was watching my little movies.

My favorites were, of course, the ones with a damsel in distress. Not in the literal sense, although historical romances were fun to watch, too. I preferred the modern ones that depicted real-life scenarios of people in love – supporting each other through their grief, carrying each other through turmoil, clinging to each other through chaos. I'd always try to picture myself in the damsel's position, allowing myself to finally feel safe enough to let someone take care of me. Or even if the roles were reversed, and the man was the one needing some saving or taking care of. I wanted to love someone enough to do that for them. I wanted to care and be cared about in return.

I looked for that in everyone, every boy I met. I'd talk to them, look them over, search for something about them to love, and tell myself, "He could be the one, could I love him?" And I probably could've, for a lot of them. But that never meant that I should. And more often than not, nothing would ever come of it anyway.

But because I thought this way, because I looked for love in everyone, I think I left a tiny piece of my heart with each and every one of them every time. It was an addiction, in a way. Both love and ROM-COM. My lifelong drug stemmed as far back as my childhood. I started to watch my life as an out-of-body experience from a third-person perspective, just like a movie would portray it. And when Madonna took me for a talk, I'd think, *this is just the part where the evil stepmother tries to stop Cinderella.* When Massimo and I played house, I'd think, *this is where Prince Charming and Cinderella dance at the ball.* And you know how movies always get to that part about halfway through when things are good, *too* good, and you know everything is going to come crashing down sooner rather than later? I'd get that feeling, too. Every time I felt okay, I knew it would come back to bite me. And it always did.

In every teen romance movie, they're always sixteen. So, at that young age, when my addiction first began, I imagined that maybe when I was sixteen, things might smooth out for me. Maybe I'd get a nice boyfriend, one that I could take home to my family and introduce to my parents like they did in the movies. Maybe we'd sit around a table for dinner and get to know each other. But when I tried to picture that table and the smiling faces around it, I couldn't see Madonna, my Dad, or my Mom. I sat there, alone, holding the hand of a ghost.

I watched all these movies on my TV, of selfless love. Prince Charming saves his princess. Rapunzel leaves the tower. Ariel gives up everything for Prince Eric. The high school drama concedes the boy gets the girl, they kiss, and a pop song plays. Playing on a loop in my childhood home, in worlds where men could still do whatever they wanted, but all they wanted was to take care of who they loved. And I wanted it to be me. I had to believe that one day, it would be *me.*

CHAPTER 4

Worse than the Birds and the Bees Talk

As I grew older, Madonna's tactics switched from passive comments to direct accusations about my mother. "Do you know what a gynecologist is?" she asked me once, casually when we were washing dishes. I was ten years old. "It's a doctor for your *down there*." I looked down and then back up at her, confused. She went on. "You know, your *vagina*. Every woman must get one at a certain age, to make sure everything is in order. Anyway. Your mom had one, of course. And you know, that's why she can only visit you once a month."

I still stared at her with blank eyes, not following. She noticed my confusion and sighed. "Oh, Cris. She had an affair with him. She cheated on your father with him." Slowly, the gears began to turn in my head. I wasn't super familiar with the concept of *cheating* or an *affair*, but it didn't sound good. She caught on and dumbed it down for me. "While she was still married to your Dad," she said, "she had sex with someone else. With her gynecologist."

My eyes widened at that. I remembered when Madonna had first taught me about sex—I was nine, she was eighteen, and she'd dragged me along to her room with her and her friends as they got ready to go out. Before she started seeing my Dad and was still only his secretary, she'd try to win me over by doing things like this. We'd sit there in her room, me gripping the headboard and swinging my feet nervously. Suddenly, she'd asked me if I knew what sex was. I'd thought about what I'd heard from the neighborhood kids and said, "It's when a man puts his hand on the chest of a woman."

Madonna laughed then. More like she cackled. It felt malicious. Her friends had laughed, too, harder than I'd seen them laugh before. "Are you that naive?" Madonna said between her chortles. "At this age, how can you not know what sex is? No, let me tell you what it *actually* is..."

She proceeded to tell me in immense detail everything she knew about sex. Now, as she said, that's what my mother had done with her *down there* doctor. I felt the heat at the base of my neck, and my face immediately flushed bright red. I quickly looked away, focusing on scrubbing the dish in my hand. She noticed my discomfort, but that didn't stop her from continuing to tell her story.

"Yeah. She was seen around town with him. While she was pregnant with your sister, too. When your parents separated and went to court, people said they saw her with him. Including your uncle, your Dad's brother, remember the one you stayed with for a while?" I didn't look up at her. I couldn't. I just hoped she'd stop talking. "I mean, that's probably why she ran away. You know she ran away, right? To Brasília, for a while. I guess she couldn't own up to her actions. That's not a real mom, just running away from the consequences. I'd never do that. If you want my honest opinion, I think she couldn't handle being a mother." Scrubbing, scrubbing, scrubbing. I couldn't get this stupid spot off the plate. "You know she married your dad when she was fifteen? Just a few years younger than I was when I got with your Dad! And she couldn't handle it! I think she just didn't want kids. But I did. She wasn't ready for it, but I always was. Isn't it so lucky for us all how these things work out?"

The plate slipped from my hand and fell to the floor with a smash, shattering. Madonna went quiet. We stared at the plate. I stiffened, waiting for her reaction.

"Cris, why did you do that?!" she demanded. "I know you did that on purpose. For attention." I tried not to flinch, waiting for the inevitable. "That's not going to work around here."

Before Madonna could say anything else, I ducked away and practically ran for the broom and dustpan to sweep the mess up. I mumbled my apologies and got to sweeping. She stood there, watching me for a moment, before walking away. I always felt like we were Cinderella and the evil stepmother. I knew she was itching to lock me away, to make sure I never met Prince Charming and never got away from her.

CHAPTER 5

Church Retreat From Hell

Despite the neighborhood kids my brother and I would regularly spend time with, I didn't feel like I had real friends. I was never an introverted kid; I'd talk to anyone who'd listen, if even just for a second. Sure, there was Massimo, the only one who'd go out of his way to acknowledge me at all. But I could tell that everyone else just tolerated me, and *barely* at that. I craved to create my own found family, friends that I could rely on, who would be there for me whenever I needed an escape from the clutches of Madonna. So, when our church hosted a youth retreat for a weekend, I made sure to go. I was lonely, and I'd take any opportunity to get out of the house and away from Madonna.

Our family was technically Catholic, but only on paper. My Dad and Madonna would never go to church, but they always made sure that my siblings and I would go at least once a week. The local church had multiple events per week—mass on Saturday evening, Sunday morning, and Sunday evening—and we had to pick at least one to go to. I usually went to more than one. But not because I cared for God, or church stuff, I liked being around people and away from my house. My relationship with God at this point was distant to say the least.

There were lots of rumors around my family, particularly about my mother, and those rumors would reflect on me. Madonna would often tell me that my mother was a slut, and no self-respecting father would ever let their daughter be my friend. By this point, my confidence was non-existent. Still, I was desperate for a friend, which may have resulted in me coming off too strong sometimes. My desperation just led to more rumors in our tremendously gossipy town.

So, when I went to the youth retreat, with a throng of other kids my age and a couple of supervisors, for a day in the countryside, it was a given that most people wouldn't talk to me. I was an outcast, ostracized by decisions that were never mine to make. Which made me question God and religion even more.

"Hey."

I looked up from my spot on the grass. I sat crisscrossed in the dirt, pulling grass out of the earth, watching the gaggle of children play a game of soccer. The "hey" had come from a boy who stood above me, freckles against his pale skin, his hair grown out in wisps around his face. He gestured to the ground next to me, asking me to sit. I shrugged. He sat.

We didn't speak much. We just kept watching the game happening in front of us. I kept pulling grass, braiding together a few loose strands. He watched my hands, and I felt his eyes on me. I didn't know if he was an introvert or if he was just bored, but I was grateful for the company regardless. At one point, he pulled some grass and tried to clumsily braid it. He clearly didn't know how. I wondered if he had any sisters.

When the day was over, and we all began to walk back to town, his friends caught up to him. I knew I'd be walking alone again on the way home. He stood in front of me in line but then suddenly turned to me.

"Your Dad owns that store in town, right?"

I nodded.

"I'll call you," he said and turned back to his friends.

I went rigid. Our phone situation was a bit weird at the moment—Dad had a storefront in town, and we'd moved into the house behind it. Our home phone was connected to the store phone, so we'd always answer for business before pleasure. And even if he did call me, there was always a chance that Madonna would be listening on the other end. Or worse, that she'd pick up the phone first.

Still, I wanted a friend. I wanted someone who *wanted* to call me. And he did. I would be stupid to pass that up.

He looked at me over his shoulder and smiled a toothy grin. I smiled back.

It wasn't worth it.

The next day, I had one of my neighborhood friends over. Not for long—I was washing dishes, making sure everything was clean before I left, and planned on changing my clothes afterward. I was twelve and just starting to care about my looks. I'd never really paid attention to them before, the same way I'd never really paid attention to boys before. But all of a sudden, it seemed like the most important thing in the world. Luckily, most of the other girls didn't mind—they were in the same boat I was.

"Cris!" I heard Madonna yell from the front of the house. I bolted toward the sound of her voice, knowing better than to keep her waiting. She stood in the doorway of the front door and gestured toward the store behind her. "Phone for you."

My heart skipped a beat. I rarely got calls. Who could it be?

I grabbed the phone from the house extension. "Hello?"

"Hey." I froze. I recognized that "hey." It was the same one I heard yesterday.

And Madonna had heard his voice. A *boy's* voice. Suddenly, I couldn't breathe.

"You there?" he said.

"I-I can't talk now." I hung up the phone, trying to swallow the lump in my throat. I turned toward the back doorway, knowing I'd see Madonna barreling in, and I hated to be right.

She grabbed my arm, her eyes ablaze, and dragged me to the bathroom in the house. Dad was in the store, too far to hear anything, although he wouldn't intervene even if he did. I knew what was coming.

"Take off your clothes," she ordered.

"Madonna, it wasn't—"

"Take. It. Off."

I obeyed, holding back my tears. Crying would only make things worse.

"You think you can just have a little boyfriend now?" she snapped. "At your age? We told you before, no dating until you graduate."

"He's not my boy—"

She smacked me in the face. I stumbled back but didn't fall. I could feel my tears spilling over now, and I was embarrassed to cry so easily. "Don't *lie*," she hissed. "You have a *boy* with your *phone number;* of course, he's your boyfriend! And you're going to lie about it too? Who *raised* you?"

"He's not! I just met him yesterday!"

She hit me again, harder, and this time I fell. I tasted blood. She leaned toward me and hit me again, and again, and again, chastising me as she did so. "Do you want to turn out like your mother?! You're well on your way there already! Your mother *lied* to your father about her affair, and now you're *lying* to me about your boyfriend! Admit it!"

I didn't. I wouldn't. There was nothing to admit. But the more I denied it, the harder she'd hit me. I sobbed, screaming over and over that there was *nothing*; he was *no one*. I felt the corner of my lips burst with blood, and as she swung at me again, I knew I'd be left with bruises on my face.

Suddenly, the front door slammed. Madonna froze. She whipped around, unlocked the door, and began looking around. "Hello? Is someone here?" she called out. I put on my clothes as quickly as I could, hoping she'd forget to beat me more if that were at all possible.

As I buttoned my pants, she stormed back in. "Did you have someone over?" she asked. Her eyes were wild as usual, but there was something else in them I wasn't used to seeing: fear and embarrassment. "Who was here?"

"My friend," I croaked out, my throat sore from crying. "She was waiting for me. We-we were going to go play outside."

The color drained from her face. "And you didn't tell me?!" she screeched. "Cris, what are people going to *think*?!"

I didn't reply. She left the bathroom for a moment and then quickly returned with cash in hand that I knew she'd gotten from the cookie jar that held our grocery money. She grabbed my face and examined the marks on it before handing me some cash.

"We're out of milk," she said. "Go to the store and buy some."

I nodded and took the money from her. She left me alone then. I looked in the mirror and inspected the damage. My lip was swollen, with blood staining the corners of my mouth. My left cheek was bright red and was already beginning to bruise beneath the surface. I touched it gingerly and immediately flinched at the pain. As I gazed in the mirror, I started to contemplate that all of this happened because of a friend I met in a church retreat. What kind of God allows something like this to happen.

I looked at the cash in my hand. I didn't understand why she was sending me out. If she was embarrassed by this, why would she send me out in public? But I wasn't going to disobey her either, so I went.

When I returned with the milk that evening, I could hear Madonna talking on the phone. Judging by the tone of her voice, it was most likely one of her close girlfriends with whom she'd often gossip. "No, no," she said nonchalantly, almost laughing. "It'll be fine. I was worried sick at first, of course. I didn't know what lies that little girl would spread about what she'd heard…No, she didn't see anything; the poor thing ran out before I even saw her! I just don't know what I'll do about Cris. She denied the whole thing! Can you believe that? Of course, I had to teach her a lesson. Do you remember what my Dad used to do to me? After he'd beat me, he'd send me out to run some errands so people could see what I deserved. A bit extreme, sure, but it made me a fast learner. I figured Cris could use some learning, too…No, think of it like this: on top of the physical discipline, there's an emotional discipline as well. It makes her ashamed of what she did…Yes, exactly. It's the *emotional* that's always gonna teach a good lesson to kids, the physical pain goes away too quick."

I'd heard enough. I closed the door behind me loud enough that I knew she'd hear, and I heard her quickly mutter her goodbyes into the phone. I headed into the kitchen to put the milk away, and she appeared before me a few seconds later. She leaned against the counter casually.

"Did you hang out with your friends?" she asked me innocently. But I knew that she just wanted to know if her tactic had worked. Even though it had somewhat worked–I saw Massimo on my way back from the store and crossed the street to avoid him, my head down–I wasn't going to give her that satisfaction. I shook my head. She frowned, disappointed.

"Okay. Well, help me make dinner. And stay around after. I want to have a talk."

I knew there was no use fighting it, so I didn't. But while we went about making dinner, I began to hatch a plan in my mind. A plan to run away.

CHAPTER 6

Time to Run Away

reathe in, breathe out. I can do this.

It was a few months later. I was 12. It had taken me that long to finally work up my nerve to act on the plan I'd started putting together a year ago. The last straw was losing the closest friends I'd ever had.

Over the past year, I'd just barely managed to steal some of my freedom back from Madonna. After finally meeting a boy who had some interest in me that extended beyond a single conversation and who was often home alone, I decided to pursue my first real relationship. Or at least, the closest thing I could imagine to a relationship. Although he wasn't Massimo, he was more convenient. His parents had meetings in the evenings, so I'd always take the opportunity to tell Madonna I was going to church when, in reality, I was going over to his place with two of our friends, the first of which I felt I could really call *friends*. When we arrived at his house, two of his friends would always be waiting there, too. It was the six of us, inseparable for that entire year.

Until the inevitable happened: the rumors of my Mom got to them. One of my friends showed up on my doorstep, looking shy and ashamed, completely unlike her. We hadn't had any plans to hang out that evening. I knew something was wrong.

"Do you want to come inside?" I offered.

She shook her head. "No, I...my Mom is waiting for me at home. I just...needed to tell you something."

I furrowed my eyebrows, trying to think of what it could be. Did she like my boyfriend? I'd always felt some tension between them. "What is it?"

She sighed, hesitant, looking down at her feet. "I can't hang out with you anymore."

Oh. This was way worse than her liking my boyfriend. "Why? Did I do something?"

Another shake of the head. "My Mom said...it's not good for us to hang out."

My heart dropped to my stomach. I knew exactly what this was about, but still, I had to ask. "Why?"

"Cris, you know why," she said, looking me in the eye for the first time, her face full of pity. "The whole *town* knows why."

Of course, I knew. But I needed to hear it. "But tell me why. What exactly did your Mom say?"

"You're not a good influence on me," she blurted out, exasperated and embarrassed at having to say it. I knew what she was referring to, that I'd turn out like my mother. It was what everyone thought.

"Do you actually believe that? That I'll turn out like my Mom?"

"I don't know, Cris." She shrugged. "Just considering your life, I guess..."

"You know more than anyone that I've never even *kissed* anyone before!" I was outraged. I thought she was one of the few people who understood me, who could look past my family's poor decisions and see that I had no control over them. But she was just like everyone else.

"Look, I have to go," she said. "My Mom—"

26 | Broken by Love: The Story of an Atheist Turned Pastor

"Yeah, I get it, she's waiting for you. Have a nice life." I slammed the door before she could get another word in. I'd just lost a friend, but I didn't feel like crying. I was angry. Angry at my Mom. For the decisions she'd made and the ones she didn't, for ruining my life because she didn't know how to manage her own. And I was especially mad at Madonna because I knew that she was the main person who went around town saying things about my Mom. She'd do anything to make herself look like a saint, and the lower she put my Mom down, the better she thought it made her look. I was never going to be anything more than the slut's daughter in this town, and it was all her fault for not keeping her stupid mouth shut.

My friend group and my relationship fell apart shortly after. I didn't reach out to anyone again—I didn't know what to say. And then I figured, and I suppose we all figured, that there was nothing else to say. Of course, they couldn't be around me. Of course, I ended up alone. I always did. The only way I could wash this label off was if I moved away from here. It was time to put my plan into action.

I packed a bag, one small enough to take it with me to school without arousing any suspicion from Madonna or any of the teachers. I shoved a change of clothes and some essentials—my toothbrush, my diary, all of my schoolwork—into my backpack and went off to school. My hope was that, to Madonna, it would look like any other normal day. That's all it was. Nothing suspicious here.

I sensed someone watching me in my room as I packed, and I whirled around to see my brother standing in the doorway like he usually did when he was bored.

I rolled my eyes. "I already told you you can't be in the girls' room–"

"Yeah, yeah." He crossed his arms. "What's up with you?"

I froze, only briefly, before zipping up my backpack. "What do you mean?"

"You were acting really weird at breakfast."

Was I really that obvious? Sometimes, I hated how well he knew me. We were very close, but we lived two different realities. Madonna treated him completely differently; he could do whatever he wanted, and he was still praised because he was a boy. But he knew how Madonna treated me our whole lives; we could see the warning signs in each other. Even without seeing any bruises on me, he could tell if Madonna had put her hands on me. He could tell if she'd kept me up the night before. And now, he could tell that I'd had enough. I tried to shake it off.

"Nothing. I'm fine." I slung my backpack over my shoulder and brushed by without looking at him. "Come on. We're gonna be late for school."

Turns out, he wasn't the only one who noticed. I was a bundle of anxiety all day. I found myself sweating all day, even when I took my sweater off. My teacher asked me twice if I was okay and even offered to send me to the nurse. I wondered if I looked pale. I shook my head and said I was fine, just a small headache. I couldn't tell if he bought it or not, but I prayed that he did. Getting caught would be detrimental; I couldn't even imagine what Madonna and my Dad would do to me.

After school, I didn't walk home like I usually would. Instead, I turned in the opposite direction and began the long walk to the other side of town. As I walked, I constantly looked over my shoulder, seeing if there was anyone who would recognize me and report to Madonna. It was such a small town I could get caught at any moment.

Twenty minutes later, I arrived at my destination in a pool of sweat. My aunt's house, my Mom's sister, the only relative from Mom's side that had the guts to still live in our town. After everything that had happened—the rumored affair, the trial, the loss of custody—Dad was ruthless. Both he and Madonna told anyone who would listen how terrible my Mom and her family were. He called them dirt—a family of immoral people. He said this of them so often that I eventually stopped seeing my Mom altogether when I was about nine years old. My brother stopped seeing her shortly after me. The only reason I even knew she was still alive was because of my little sister, who never gave up and consistently kept her monthly visits with our mother. I both envied and admired her for this.

So now, as I stood in front of my aunt's house, it struck me just how long it had been since I last saw her. Three years? Maybe four? How would she react? Did she even want to see me? Was I welcome here?

Just as I was considering turning around and running back home, the front door opened. A woman stepped out, her hair short and dark, her face fresh and young. She squinted at me as if I were a mirage, and she didn't quite trust her vision.

"Cristiane?" she asked. The moment I nodded, tears sprang to her eyes, and a part of me felt somewhat repulsed. This wasn't supposed to be a sentimental moment; I just needed to get away.

She ran over to me and pulled me into the tightest hug I'd ever felt. I could barely breathe. She sobbed into my shoulder, wetting my shirt, but I didn't care. I was finally wanted by someone, and that was all that mattered.

She ushered me inside, blabbing the whole way. "Are you staying for lunch? I was just finishing making food for myself, but I'll make more for you. How are you? Did you just get out of school? You're so thin, have you been eating? I'm going to feed you well today, don't you worry! I have rice and beans, lots of bread, and some juice. What kind of juice do you like? I have some options for you!"

I couldn't stop smiling. I tried to remember the last time I'd ever been treated this well in my entire life, and I couldn't recall a single moment. Why had I suffered with Madonna for so long when my aunt's doors had always been open to me? How could I have ever believed I wasn't wanted here? What was I so afraid of?

She didn't ask me what I was doing there or if my Dad knew I was there. She just fed me, and talked, and laughed, and cried. And so, I didn't bring it up, or the fact that I was running away. Everything seemed so small compared to this wonderful point in time. I just ate, talked, laughed, and cried along with her.

But I hadn't looked over my shoulder enough in my walk earlier because someone inevitably reported a sighting of me to Madonna. I don't know who saw me or where, but it didn't take long for my Dad and Madonna to pull up in their car in front of the house. I was more shocked to see my Dad there than anything else; he was usually working at this time. Madonna must have called him for backup, and I knew he'd take any opportunity to tell me again what a monster my mother was.

They opened the car door and got out but didn't move toward the house. They stood there, waiting for me, treating my aunt's home as if it were under quarantine.

"*Cris!*" Dad yelled from his spot by the car. "Come outside! *Now!*"

I looked at my aunt, frozen. I knew my eyes were pleading, but I didn't know what I was asking for. She seemed to be pleading with me, too. But neither of us would vocalize what we wanted. So I stood up from the table and went outside.

The car was only a few steps away, so I walked as slowly as possible, saying over and over again in my head to stick

30 | Broken by Love: The Story of an Atheist Turned Pastor

with my plan. *You're not going home. You're staying here. Or you're moving in with Mom. But you're not. Going. Home. Don't do it. Don't give in.*

I stopped a few feet away from my Dad. He stepped closer, looming over me. He was never the type to try and get down on my level and see eye-to-eye the way I'd seen other fathers do. He stood with his back straight, hands on his hips, trying to look as big as possible. And it definitely worked. Still, I preferred to look at him than at Madonna, who I was sure was giving me a death stare. If I went home, I was sure she'd keep me up until 5 am that night.

"What are you doing, Cris?" he said. He didn't sound angry; he sounded disappointed, which was worse. He somehow managed to keep his cool, which was even scarier than his usual outrage.

As he asked me that question, I thought about how long I'd had this plan. I thought about the wonderful lunch I just had. I thought about how I don't even know what my mother looks like anymore. And I wanted to know so badly. But no matter what I wanted; I couldn't stop the following words from coming out of my mouth: "I don't know."

It was the truth, in a way. I didn't know what I was doing. I didn't know what it would be like to live with Mom, whether it would be better or worse, although I couldn't imagine anything worse than Madonna. Regardless, the fear had frozen me, and it was difficult to hold on to the motivation that led me to my aunt's house in the first place.

"Do you know who these people are?" he asked me. I knew it was a rhetorical question, so I didn't answer. He went on, his voice louder. "They're the lowest of the low. They're *immoral* people, Cris. Is that really what you want to be involved with? You want to become like your *mother*?"

"She'd be lucky to turn out like her mother!"

I whipped my head around to see my aunt still standing by the front door. She was within earshot, and I knew she'd heard every word. She was crying again, but this time, they were angry tears. Her hands shook with rage. "God forbid she ever turns out like *you*! Or worse, like your trampy girlfriend!"

My Dad didn't acknowledge her. He just looked at me and pointed at her. "You see that? Is that really how you want to turn out?"

"*Leave!*" my aunt screeched as loud as she could. "Get away from here! You've already harassed the rest of my family enough! Let us live in peace!"

My Dad put one hand on my shoulder and used the other to open the door to the backseat. "She's insane. I don't want you engaging with those types of people. Get in, let's go home."

I couldn't tear my eyes away from my aunt. She *did* look crazy. But I wondered whether her supposed insanity was her own fault or my father's.

Still, I knew what I had to do. I got in the car and let him close the door behind me. We drove home in silence. Although Madonna had been mostly quiet the entire time, I knew I wouldn't hear the end of it later that night.

The moment I got home, and my brother and I were alone, he turned to me. "You tried, didn't you?"

I shrugged, too exhausted and embarrassed to get into it. "I don't know what you mean."

"You *know* what type of person Mom is." He scowled at me. "Yeah, it sucks here, but do you really want to do that to Dad?"

"I didn't *do* anything," I insisted.

"Yeah? Then where were you all afternoon?"

"With a friend."

He rolled his eyes. "Please. We both know you don't have a lot of those."

"Whatever." I pushed past him to my room. "I'm not in the mood."

"You're just gonna turn out like her if you keep trying!" he called after me. I didn't turn around, didn't reply. I wondered how often Dad told him that to make him believe it. I wondered when I started believing too.

CHAPTER 7

Betrayed by the One Closest to Me

It didn't take long for the story of my little escapade to reach the rest of the neighborhood. Massimo was still the only one who was nice to me, so on a surface level, nothing seemed out of the ordinary. But I saw the way the kids started looking at me. Noticed the way they'd get quiet when I showed up. Watched them through my window, going to get ice cream with no intention of telling me. It especially became noticeable when my brother started going out without me.

Normally, we'd go outside together. He'd do the thing he always does, stand in the doorway of my room and wait. But soon enough, my only signal that we were going out was the sound of the door slamming shut, telling me he was already gone.

It all came to a head one day when my brother had long gone out without me realizing. It was a hot day, and I knew everyone would be out by the food trucks in the plaza, getting ice cream. I raced over while thinking about what I could do to regain my position in the group. I knew they never liked me that much, but I'd never been so excluded.

I heard their laughter coming from the picnic tables set up outside the ice cream truck. I slowed my pace, trying to catch my breath and not make it so obvious how desperate I was for their company. But I stopped in my tracks entirely when I heard my name.

"It's so stupid! Why would she try to go in the first place?" a boy's voice asked.

"Probably because she wants to be a slut like her Mom," I heard my brother say. I was behind the ice cream truck, hidden from view, and I peered around the corner. He was licking his ice cream casually as he said this, his mouth sticky and sweet like a child, but his words were that of a man's. They were our father's words. "They're crazy people. And Cris is just like them."

My face felt hot with anger and betrayal. I was so distracted by my brother that I didn't notice Massimo's eyes on me. He sat at the table, ice cream dripping down his hand, watching me. He didn't move, didn't speak, didn't give me away. His eyes were full of sympathy for me. Maybe even pity. I turned and ran home.

The moment I heard my brother's footsteps return that afternoon, I cornered him.

"A slut like her Mom?!" I said, angry and not trying to hide it. "Are you *serious*?"

He seemed caught off guard, but only for a moment before collecting himself. "What, are you eavesdropping on me now?"

I hated him more for not even trying to deny it. Was he not at all ashamed? "How long have you been saying that about me?" I asked. And suddenly, it dawned on me, and I was furious. "Is that why my friend told me she couldn't hang out with me anymore? Is that why my boyfriend broke up with me?!"

"If they did all that, it's probably because they can tell that you're like Mom," he said bluntly. His tone reminded me of Madonna's. "Doesn't mean I had anything to do with it."

"Liar! They all hate me now! This is because of *you!*"

"Cris, *everyone* knows who you are and who you're gonna be! It's not a secret! I'm just–"

"Just what? Carrying out Madonna's dirty work?"

He glared at me. "*No.* I'm just *warning* them. You know what Dad always says–"

"What? Does *he* say that about me, too?"

"No. But…" he shrugged again. "He knows what the risks are. Especially if you go back to Mom."

"Who said *anything* about going back to Mom?!"

"You tried to run away to her, Cris!"

"Can you blame me?!" How could he not get it? I thought he'd suffered as much as I had with Madonna – but that is when I started realizing that he didn't. "With what we go through here–"

"So, you'd rather have *that* reputation than deal with Madonna?"

"Maybe I would! Maybe–maybe it's better than this!"

He didn't say anything for a moment. He just gave me a pointed look as if my statement proved his point. He turned to go to the kitchen. "And that's *exactly* what I'm warning them about.

CHAPTER 8

This Time Has to Work

"But I *want them!*"

I wanted a pair of sandals, and I didn't care what it would take to get it. While exploring the town with my friends the other day, I saw the most glorious pair of sandals through a storefront window. Bright pink, like every little girl loved, with plastic rhinestones sewn into its straps. I knew I was made for them, and I made sure my Dad knew it.

He wasn't home often—he worked very long hours—leaving us subject to the whims of Madonna, who I wouldn't dare ask for anything. But he was around that day, and I thought it was perfect timing. However, my asking had quickly turned to pleading when Dad immediately said no when I first asked.

"Cris, sometimes we can't have the things we want, okay?" he told me. "That's how life is."

But I wasn't having it. I began to cry, pouting. "But *why not?*"

"Because I said so, Cris! I don't need another reason!"

And then the idea struck me. I knew how to hit him where it hurt, even if it was a lie. "If you don't buy it for me," I yelled, "I'm gonna go live with Mom!"

Dad froze, then. His face dropped. I couldn't read his eyes, but they bore into me, and I was terrified; I'd never seen him look at me like that.

He bent down on his knee to reach my level, which he never did, and stared me right in the eye. "If you ever say that again," he said, his words laced with venom, "I will hit you."

I didn't say anything. I was too afraid and stunned by the way he looked at me. He said, "Do you understand?" And I nodded. It was all I could do.

He straightened up and walked away. Dad had always said mean things about Mom, although I honestly believed he didn't realize when he did it. He'd say Mom's family was immoral, below us, and he doesn't want us to ever be on that level. But at this moment, I learned and fully understood that the worst offense in the world was to favor her over Dad.

I remembered this interaction that happened when I was 7 or 8 when I was thirteen and had just moved in with Mom for the first time. Unlike the first time I tried to run away, I didn't quite plan this one out.

When it was time for the monthly visit with Mom, Madonna would ask me if I wanted to go. I knew she was testing me, so I'd always say no. When summer vacation came around, Mom had the right to spend half of the summer with us. This was something I'd reject every time as well. But this year, as summer vacation approached, something came over me.

I sat on the couch watching TV after school, which was my usual routine. Madonna came in.

"Do you want to visit your Mom this summer?" She asked it so casually that I knew she didn't think anything of it by now. She expected me to say no; it wasn't really a question anymore. And this, on top of my brother's accusations, made me angrier than I thought it would.

So, trying to mimic her casual tone as much as I could, I said, "Sure."

Although she was standing a few feet away from me, I could still sense her stiffening. I tried to keep my breathing steady. *I won't panic. I won't give in.*

"Are...are you *sure* you want to do that?" she said, the shock evident in her voice.

"Yeah," was all I said in response.

I finally stood up and looked at her, grabbing my plate of snacks as if I were about to bring it to the kitchen, but I froze in my tracks once I saw her face: red with anger, her lips pursed, and her eyebrows furrowed. She had a silly face when she was angry. I would've laughed if I weren't so afraid. I stiffened, prepared for her to lash out, but she turned and stormed out instead.

I knew immediately that she was going to get my Dad, who was working in the store out front. She left the door wide open and yelled as she spoke to my Dad, clearly wanting me to hear her. "*Your daughter* wants to go *visit* her *mother* this summer!" she announced. I heard a low rumble in response, Dad's voice. Her voice cut short, and I heard pounding footsteps approaching the house. I knew that once I said I wanted to visit Mom, he'd come storming in eventually to ask me what I could possibly be thinking. But I wasn't prepared to face him so soon. I adjusted my position, rolling my shoulders back and straightening my posture to look as mature yet nonchalant as possible. This was it. I just had to stay strong.

Dad stomped in, Madonna following closely behind. I managed to maintain eye contact with them both, just barely. *Breathe, breathe, breathe.*

I waited for his words or for Madonna's hand to hit me. The three of us stood there, breathing heavily, waiting for someone to make a move. The tension in the air was thick.

But my Dad didn't say anything. He just stared. He looked like he wanted to kill me. And then he turned and walked out, slamming the door as he left.

"Do you know what this is doing to him?" Madonna said immediately. "Just the *thought* of you going? It's *killing* him, Cris."

This caught me off guard, and for a moment, my facade slipped. "What do you mean?"

She scoffed. "Don't play dumb! You know *exactly* what you're doing! It's like you enjoy torturing him!"

"I-I don't," I said, cursing myself for stuttering. I tried again but couldn't get any more words to come out.

"You haven't seen her in years for good reason! You know the type of person she is!"

I didn't reply because the truth was, I didn't know. I only knew what they'd told me, what the town said. But in reality, my mother was a stranger to me.

"If he has a heart attack and dies," she spat at me, "it'll be *your* fault. *You'll* be the one who killed him."

Before I could panic in front of her, she left again, stomping her feet so hard that I could feel the vibrations on the floor and hear picture frames rattling. I put my hand on my chest to calm myself. *Breathe, breathe, breathe.* And I prayed it would all be worth it. It had to be.

My brother was the next to confront me a few days later as I packed all my things. He stood in the doorway of the girls' room again, the same way he used to. I couldn't remember the last time he did that. I didn't get upset at him this time; I just ignored him and focused on packing. But he knew I could sense his presence.

"Are you seriously going?" he asked.

I shrugged. "Why not?"

"Seriously?" He scoffed. "I guess I was right to warn everyone about you. You really are gonna turn out just like her."

I looked up at the ceiling, willing myself not to cry. "I just...I can't be here anymore, okay? And it's not like you made it any easier for me.

"I only said what I said to everyone because I knew you'd do this eventually," he said. "We all knew."

"How could you know when I didn't even know myself? This wasn't *planned*. I've just...had enough."

"Madonna said you're gonna kill Dad." My breath became heavy. It felt like the air was sucked out of the room. "She said you don't care if he dies. Is that true?"

"Of course not," I said. "But you don't believe me anyway, do you?"

"Not if you go with your mom for the vacation break."

"Well, I'm going, so…"

"Okay then."

I looked at him for the first time. He was trying to keep his face neutral, but I could see the rage in his eyes. And along with the rage, sadness. And betrayal. I knew that he would always be on my Dad's side, and from his perspective, if I wasn't with him, I was against him. I wished he could understand that I wasn't on anyone's side anymore. I was on my *own* side for once.

CHAPTER 9

The Other Side of the Story

Goiânia was much bigger than Olímpia. In Olímpia, everyone knew everyone. You could walk through the entire town in just a few minutes. The only thing to do on a Saturday night was sit by the food trucks in the town square. Where Olímpia felt empty, Goiânia felt full.

My mother lived in an apartment on the top floor. Throughout the time we lived in Goiania she managed several buildings throughout the city. When I first moved there, she was the manager of a commercial high-rise by the name of Empire State. There was a huge university nearby, and the building we lived in held various college kids. Usually, four of them packed into a two-bedroom. I could hear them clambering the staircase late at night, the music emanating from their living rooms into the halls. I was 13. This was where I ended up for the summer.

Although I left because I couldn't deal with Madonna anymore, I quickly realized that living with Mom wasn't too much of an improvement either. Especially since I was shocked and disappointed to find out some of Madonna's brainwashing had actually worked on me.

"I told you, *that didn't happen!*" Mom yelled, frustrated with having to repeat herself for the millionth time. She stood in the living room, having gotten up from her seat due to the heated conversation. I lay stretched out on the couch, but that didn't stop me from talking back.

"That's not what *the whole town* said!" I yelled back. I thought her to be a liar. "There were witnesses! They saw you!"

"*Fake* witnesses!" she shot back. "And how would you know? You weren't even in the courtroom; you were a child! You still are! The only things you know are what *Madonna* told you. Do you really believe that?"

"I believe that you left because you didn't know how to be a mother! And you *still* don't!"

"Oh, did Madonna tell you that?!"

I sat up. "Yeah! And she also said the town thinks you're a call girl!"

Her jaw dropped. "*Cris!* I will not be talked to like that in *my own house!*"

"Fine!"

"Fine!"

She stormed off to her room. I heard the door slam and flinched. I sighed and laid back down, picking up my bowl of ramen that I'd neglected. We had a maid to cook for us regularly. However, when it came to evenings and weekends, I had to make my own food, so ramen became my best friend. I twirled the noodles with my fork, blowing the steam off before taking a bite.

Truth be told, I wasn't sure why I treated her the way I did. Did I actually feel that way toward her? Did I think she was a call girl? Did I think she had an affair with her gynecologist while she was pregnant with my sister? I wasn't sure anymore. But it was all I'd been told for so long that it was like those theories were engraved in my brain, and now that I was around my mother, the only thing I knew to do was regurgitate what I'd been taught. What I'd been *trained*. Maybe Madonna really was a good psychologist. She could have a bright future as a hypnotist.

The next day, over lunch, when both of us had cooled off, we sat at the dining room table. Mom started. "Your Grandma told me to leave," she said suddenly. I pushed the food around on my plate, barely interested. "Your Dad...wasn't the best husband to me. He was always a bit verbally abusive, as I'm sure you know. Sometimes...rarely, but sometimes physical." I remembered the bruises I'd once seen on my Mom's neck. Only once. Still, I wasn't sure I believed her. I stayed quiet and listened anyway.

"I thought your Grandma was looking out for me," she continued. "Your Dad started accusing me of cheating, even though he was the one who'd flirt with women right in front of me." She scoffed. "Anyway, your Grandma said that trying to take care of our relationship would end up killing me. I was exhausted; everyone could see it. She told me I needed to leave the kids with her, stay away for a while, and come back when things calmed down. And I had a friend in Brasília, so...I left. I got a job. I worked and saved money. And then I came back."

She looked at me then, her eyes gentle and wet. "I was always going to come back, Cris. It was only three months, I never meant to—I was never going to abandon you."

"So..." I finally spoke. "What happened when you came back?"

She sighed shakily; and quickly wiped her eyes, staring up at the ceiling. I took a sip of my drink as I waited. It was starting to get darker, and a yellow lamp was the only light we kept on in the living room. It reflected on her face, casting eerie yet comforting shadows. "Well...I was too late. It was like everyone was suddenly against me. Your Dad built a case while I was gone, so I was completely caught off guard and

44 | Broken by Love: The Story of an Atheist Turned Pastor

under prepared. He'd gotten the whole town on his side got his brother to be a fake witness. I didn't stand a chance."

Whether she was telling the truth or not, I knew she was right about one thing: she didn't stand a chance. I remember my Dad telling my little brother, over and over again, "Men can do whatever they want." He never said that to me. In the 80's, a small town, in the interior of Brazil, it was rare for a woman to be believed, let alone in a court case. My Mom was young, naive, and afraid. My Dad was older, good-looking, charming, and friends with the best lawyers and the judge. It was no contest.

This was the first time that I began to see my paternal grandma in a different light as well. I always had the fondest memories of her—she spoiled me rotten. When I was 10, she'd still bring me chocolate milk in a baby bottle every morning. Although childish, at the time, it was the best thing in the world to wake up with a sweet taste in my mouth. It was one of the few pleasant memories I had from childhood. Now, years later, those memories took on a distorted shape.

But as I sat there, listening to my Mom tell her side of the story for the first time, it was difficult to feel bad for her. How *stupid* could she be? In the middle of a court case to get custody of your kids, and you *leave*? No wonder things turned out the way they did. No wonder she lost everything.

It was then I decided that no matter who was telling the truth about the story, Madonna was right about one thing. My Mom didn't try hard enough. A part of her, no matter how small, wanted to lose that court case. She was only 25—she wanted to start over without a husband, without kids, without us, without *me*. And when I put my anger aside, I understood. I was unwanted, yes, but I understood why.

June went by quickly. Besides a few arguments with my mother, I barely remember the month at all. I didn't really talk to anyone or make many friends yet, but I was enamored with the college kids who haunted our halls. They seemed so grown-up, so effortlessly cool. I wanted to be like them. So by the end of the month, my hands shaking as I journeyed back to Olímpia, I knew I'd already made up my mind.

I was terrified seeing my father approach me in the courthouse. I couldn't tell if he looked different or if maybe I just wasn't used to seeing him after a month. I reminded myself to breathe slowly, speak slowly, and stay calm.

We'd left Goiânia and driven straight to the courthouse in Olímpia. I didn't want to go home–I was afraid Madonna would corner me, convince me to give in and change my mind. Instead, we told my Dad to meet us there. I was determined: I was going to move in with my mother and grant her full custody.

He walked right up to me without looking at my mother. He towered over me. I could see his nostrils flare. "Are you sure you want to do this?" he asked.

I swallowed hard, Madonna's and my brother's voices ringing in my ears. *You're going to kill him.* Still, I managed to find the strength to nod but didn't speak for fear of my voice trembling.

He nodded back at me, his face hard. And then he turned and walked into the courtroom. My mother and I shared a glance before trailing behind.

I didn't have a lot, so most of my things were already at my Mom's place. I didn't want to go back to my Dad's home in Olímpia, so I convinced myself I could survive without the rest of my things. I wanted to leave everything behind and get a fresh start. I had the opportunity to recreate myself–to be known as something other than the slut's daughter, to be out-going and fun, to have the friends I always wanted. Goiânia was going to be different. It had to be.

The trial took only a month. By August, my mother was granted full custody, and I'd already moved in permanently with her. School was about to start, and there was a private Catholic school nearby that my mother quickly enrolled me in. And so, my life in Goiânia began.

It was a mess from the start.

CHAPTER 10

Things Will Be Different Now

"Oh, you cleaned the stove!"

My mother's surprise and praise irked me. I didn't know exactly why, but almost everything about her annoyed me. I wasn't really interested in having a good or even remotely amicable relationship with her. Despite having some understanding of why she did the things she did, it was difficult to undo Madonna's years of brainwashing. Plus, I quickly picked up on my mother's habit of victimizing herself. Sure, she had it rough. But where was the accountability for her mistakes?

While living with Madonna and my Dad, I felt like Cinderella before she was a princess. Constantly cleaning everything, running around, waiting on every one hand and foot. I was used to cleaning in my free time and continued this habit in the early days of living with my mother. But once I saw her surprise and realized that this wasn't expected of me, I stopped immediately. She had a maid already, and the apartment was small–what did she need me for? I started leaving my dirty dishes in the sink. Instead of doing my own laundry, I left it in the hamper. When I got home from school, I'd eat whatever the maid had cooked and then watch TV on the couch until I fell asleep. I'd gone from being the pauper to the princess. It was *my* turn to be waited on.

48 | Broken by Love: The Story of an Atheist Turned Pastor

In my mind, I had the perfect routine. Whenever I woke up from my nap in the late afternoon, I'd venture out to see what adventures awaited me that day. I was like a restless puppy that had been kept in its cage for too long. Madonna always held me back from making any close friendships, and my mother's reputation, on top of that, always scared off potential friendships. Now, I was unchained. I wanted to do everything and see everything.

Where I'd once had no friends at all, I now had various friend groups to choose from. I fell into a clique of kids at school, and also befriended a couple of college kids in my building. I didn't think about what I was doing anymore; I just did it, excited to have the freedom to do anything at all.

I knocked on the door of Carlos and Davi's apartment. They were two brothers in college, both of them nearly 20 years old, while I was still 13. Davi opened the door and smiled when he saw me. "Cris! Come on in."

I grinned. I'd never say it out loud, but he was my favorite of the two.

His apartment was typical for a college guy—not many decorations, sparse furniture, bottles, and ashtrays littering tables. The constant smell of beer and weed that singed my nostrils. I had to fight the urge to scrunch my nose, not wanting to seem childish in front of them. I liked them because I thought they treated me like one of them; I felt grown up around them.

They had parties often, and another was just beginning to start that day. It was my first time attending, and I didn't really know what to expect. I only knew what I'd seen in movies—the plastic cups, the crowded rooms of bodies dancing against each other, the dim lights. But here, the lights were fully on. There were no plastic cups, just the usual beer bottles. Although the crowd was about what I expected, most of them were lounging around instead of dancing. Leaning against the kitchen counter, stretched across the couch, some even sitting on the floor. Music blasted from the speakers, causing everyone to yell over one another to just barely hold a conversation. I examined the faces of all the 18-20-year olds, wondering if I was the youngest one there. Wondering if they could see my youngness, my naivety, on my face.

A beer found its way into my hand. I looked up at Carlos, who was handing it to me. He put a finger to his lips and winked at me. "Don't tell your Mom, alright? But I figured your first drink should be in the company of friends."

Friends. It felt right at the time that these people could be my friends. I thought they liked me for me. Of course, I'd only see the truth years down the line: that they were waiting for the opportunity to strike, to take advantage of a kid. I didn't see predators when I looked at them; I saw the companionship I'd desired for so long.

The night went on. One beer turned into two, turned into three, I think. I wasn't sure anymore. Regardless, I found myself squished into the corner of the couch, a guy who looked around Davi's age chatting me up. His mouth was close to me, yelling loudly over the music. I still couldn't hear what he was saying. I couldn't remember how this conversation started. His breath was hot. If I looked straight ahead, I'd be looking straight into his mouth. I tried to smile and nod and laugh at what seemed like the right moments.

Someone tried to squeeze past us and bumped into his leg. He eyed them up and down before turning back to me. He nodded toward the hall that led to the bedrooms. I focused on reading his lips to understand his next words. "Do you wanna go somewhere quieter?"

I blushed and nodded. This was it. This was what always happened in the movies. The cute guy asks the girl to go somewhere quiet, and they talk the rest of the night, away from the party and the noise. Maybe even share a kiss. It seemed so romantic, and I wanted a whirlwind romance like the ones I always saw on TV. This seemed like my way of getting that.

The music was muffled behind the bedroom door. He sat on the bed, leaning against the headboard, and I followed, curling my legs up beneath me, feeling incredibly shy and self-conscious. How did these things normally go? How did they start?

He put his hand on my leg. I smiled. *This is how it starts.*

Nothing happened. No thanks to my stupidity.

As he leaned into me, I realized how terrified I actually was. My butterflies transformed into just plain old nausea, and I wanted his hands off of me. Was I ready to have sex? With a guy I just met? Suddenly, I wasn't so sure. I tried to backtrack, but he wasn't listening. He kept touching me, leaning in, I felt like I couldn't breathe. So I bolted. I rushed out of the party without saying goodbye to anyone, stumbling up the stairs to my Mom's apartment. Even though nothing happened, I was still mortified. *The little thirteen-year-old is too afraid for a college party. Typical.*

Regardless, I was sure that Davi and Carlos must've heard differently. The guy probably already started a rumor that I *did* sleep with him, and Davi and Carlos wouldn't want anything to do with me anymore. Although there was no proof of this, I was so used to being looked at as someone promiscuous that I was too embarrassed to visit them again. It felt like the same situation I'd had with my ex-boyfriend and ex-friends. *"Sorry, can't hang out with a slut!"* Of course, that would happen to me—it always did.

I didn't see any of them often, despite living in the same building. Goiânia was big enough, and we had such different schedules that it was easy to avoid them. And I had enough friends by then that I didn't mind leaving behind a few. If I messed up with one friend, I had another waiting for me. Resolving any misunderstandings wasn't a necessity anymore; I could just move on instead.

Naturally, this wasn't the best option for my mental state. It probably wouldn't be good for anyone's mental state, but mine was particularly fragile. After the party situation, I found myself crying in the stairwell, day after day. At first, I thought it was just because I had lost my friendship with Carlos and Davi. But the tears wouldn't stop. Things were not that different, I found myself crying daily, almost routinely, oftentimes without even knowing why.

"What's wrong?" I look up to see Willis ascending the staircase, grocery bags in hand. I'd started spending more time with him, another collegial resident in the apartment building. We'd met back in June when I first visited my Mom, but I didn't see him often until I started having my daily cries. He found me like this regularly, my face puffy and red. I was embarrassed the first time he saw me, but now I was used to it. He was never judgmental about it. He'd do the same thing every time: set his groceries down, sit next to me on the staircase, and let me rest my head on his shoulder. Sometimes, we'd sit there in silence; sometimes, we'd talk for hours. Regardless, after a few minutes, he'd stand up and reach for my hand. We'd walk, hand-in-hand, up the stairs to his apartment, where he'd let me lay on his couch as he cooked dinner.

I saw the way he looked at me. I knew that he wanted more from our relationship than I was willing to give him. We'd date on and off, but I never felt secure enough to call him my boyfriend. I didn't know how to take a relationship seriously, and I cared about Willis too much to risk anything serious. I saw him as a guardian angel of sorts–he was about 4 years older than me, stronger, he looked like John Travolta, tall, with dark hair and piercing blue eyes. I couldn't believe that someone like him would even look at me, and he always showed up when I needed him. He was the youngest of seven brothers, so I assumed he was tired of being taken care of and wanted to take care of me instead. But whenever things were going well between us, I'd ruin it. I'd kiss someone else, break up with him, and/or cry again. I couldn't stay in place. I was always looking for something new, some new adventure, something to do. He couldn't keep up. Honestly? I could barely keep up with myself.

CHAPTER 11

I was Out of Control

Neither could my mother, for that matter. After everything I'd been through with Madonna, I found myself going crazy with my newfound freedom, and even crazier when it was attempted to be controlled. I'd go out for days at a time and wouldn't bother coming home–too busy binge drinking with friends from my new school and crashing at their place. I never called my Mom whenever I did that. I had the opportunity to do so because, of course, there was always a phone at my friend's house, but I *wanted* her to worry. Not only that, but I wanted to hurt her. Yeah, if I put my anger aside, I could understand her side of everything that had happened. But she was still a coward, and my understanding didn't mean I'd made my peace with it. I still hated her, and in a messed-up way, I wanted her to pay for the way she'd treated me.

My new stepdad, a guy she'd met in Brasília when she ran away from us, always pushed her to put me in line. It made me hate him, too. On one of their many failed attempts, after I disappeared for yet another weekend, my Mom locked me in my room, thanks to the counsel of my stepdad, and yelled through the door that she wasn't going to let me out for the rest of the day. I was *not* having it *at all.*

54 | Broken by Love: The Story of an Atheist Turned Pastor

I pounded on the door and tried jiggling the doorknob time and time again for the first 20 minutes. Once it was clear that she really wasn't going to let me out, I went to the wall next to the door. It wasn't made of brick or concrete, but it was firm, and I knew that the sound would reverberate throughout the apartment if I hit it hard enough. I placed my hands against the wall and braced myself before I slammed my head against it as hard as I could.

"*Cris*, what are you *doing*?!" I heard my Mom yell as soon as I first made impact. I hit my head against it twice more for good measure. She banged on the door. "*Cris!* What is that noise?!"

"Giving myself a concussion!" I yelled back and slammed my head again. It hurt, but I didn't care. I just wanted to get out. "You'll have to unlock the door to take me to the hospital soon!"

"Stop being dramatic!" she said. I scoffed. Drama? She doesn't know the half of it.

I went over to my bedroom window, opened it up, and looked over the ledge. We were on the 10th floor of this apartment building, and it was a long way down. But I was crazed and careless.

"I'll jump!" I threatened, screaming at the top of my lungs. "I opened the window! I'll jump *right now*!"

"*Cris, enough!*" she said, and the doorknob jiggled. I could tell she was tempted to open it, but I could hear my stepfather speaking in a low voice, encouraging her not to give in to my insanity. I scowled. He ruined everything.

I swung one leg over the edge. "My leg is out the window!" I called out. "I'm going to jump!"

"No, you're not!" my stepdad spoke to me for the first time through the door. "Stop being dramatic! You need to grow up!"

"I'm gonna count to five," I screamed hysterically, "and then I'm jumping!"

I heard my Mom and stepdad bickering behind the door, going back and forth between themselves as they tried to decide whether or not they should come in. I start counting.

"*One!*"

The door swung open, and both of their eyes widened when they saw me sitting on the ledge, my leg still hanging outside. The wind ruffled my hair, stronger than usual all the way up here. I wondered if my forehead was still red from banging it against the wall.

"*Cris*, are you *crazy?!*" She began to walk towards me, but my stepdad reached out with his arm and held her back.

He approached me slowly, as if I were a wild animal. In a way, I was.

"Cris," he said in a low voice. "Come back over the ledge."

"Will you let me out?" I asked. I grabbed the ledge with my hands, ready to push myself off if I needed to.

"Cristiane–"

"Will you *let me out?!*" I demanded.

"No!" His face was bright red and sweaty with stress. "Enough!"

"I'd rather *die* than let you keep me in here!"

He stopped in his tracks and took a deep breath. Yes, it was dramatic, but it was true. I would've rather died than be controlled, and I meant it. They could tell I meant it, too.

"Yes," my Mom cut in, tears in her eyes. "Yes, yes, we'll let you out."

A week later, the window was bolted shut.

CHAPTER 12

Strange Religious Beliefs

My family was technically Catholic, but that was only on a surface level. If you looked deeper, particularly into my family history, you'd find some... interesting things.

When I was six years old, when my Mom and Dad were still together–before everything fell apart–my Mom took me to what she said was her friend's son's birthday party. She said her son was about my age, and there'd be other kids there. Maybe I'd get along with them. Maybe I'd make some friends. And since I was desperate for company, even at such a young age, I didn't hesitate to go along with her.

She definitely exaggerated the number of kids that would be there. It was a handful, maybe five. The room was mostly full of adults, mingling and drinking. I talked to a few of the kids, but every time I asked who the birthday boy was, nobody knew. I didn't think as much about it as I should've–I figured he was an introvert, or maybe they were new to town, so he didn't know anyone here. I brushed it aside as I played with the other kids until it was time to sing Happy Birthday, and the topic was unavoidable.

They brought out the cake with candles and began to sing as the birthday boy's mother brought it to the table. The other kids and I approached, curious to finally see him. But when we looked at the table all we saw was a bunch of framed photos of a little boy sitting on the edge of the table, and candles surrounding his various faces. I looked around to catch my mother's eye but found her singing along with all the other adults like it was perfectly normal.

I later found out that the boy had passed away a while ago. But it was being celebrated as if he were still there, with us.

These types of things were normal to my mother. There were a lot of spiritists in Brazil, and my mother's family was especially full of believers. I didn't know exactly what to make of them. I'd gotten used to Catholicism, but spiritualism felt foreign, and a bit strange. It wasn't scary to me at all; just uncomfortable.

So now, at 13, I shifted in my seat awkwardly as a man swung a pendulum around me. My Mom had brought me here as yet another attempt to discipline me or at least figure out what I was up to. And the worst part was that she hung back as he took me into a separate room. She just left me alone with some weird guy I'd never seen before! And he was starting to creep me out with his shaky voice and this weird-looking pendulum.

"Are you a virgin?" he asked suddenly, still waving around his pendulum, and I was immediately even more creeped out.

"Um...yes," I said.

"Do you drink? Or smoke?"

"Why are you asking me this?"

He closed his eyes and took a deep breath, not responding. I assumed he was waiting for my answer.

"No," I lied. "No, I don't."

He asked me more questions, and I figured out that it was some sort of lie detector test. Or at least, that's what he believed it to be. It clearly didn't work, and I started to find it a bit funny. With his whole hippie look, and how he was so

58 | Broken by Love: The Story of an Atheist Turned Pastor

into this pendulum. Did he actually believe this? Did my *Mom* actually believe this?

He continued with the questions for about half an hour, and I lied more often than not. When my Mom finally came back into the room, I was less uncomfortable and more amused. This was stupid and clearly a waste of everyone's time. But if he believed in my lies and told her everything I said, then maybe she'd at least get off my back for a few days, and I could take advantage of it.

I took maybe a little too much advantage. But in my defense, I got carried away with all the festivities in town.

There's a rodeo in Goiânia that lasts for a full week every year, and this was my first one since it was my first time living with my Mom during this time of year. I went with a friend, who told me it was *the* event to be at. I was surprised by how many others in my school and apartment building were anticipating it. But as we walked up to the street that it was all taking place on; I immediately understood it was for the drinking.

Every bar in town had their own tents set up, lining the streets as far as you could see. It was a major celebration, and celebrations called for drinks. The whole town was looking forward to getting drunk all week long, so every tent was packed. Empty beer bottles and spilled cups littered the streets. Everyone we talked to would mention some afterparty or another. The whole week seemed to be lined up with parties. It was *perfect* for 13-year-old me, a breeding ground for chaos. At one of these tents, a beer in hand while my friend chatted some boys up about yet another afterparty, I met Jonas. Or, as he was better known by his friends, the Devil. Just my luck.

It was a perfect nickname for someone like him. Tall, dark hair, and the biggest trouble I'd ever encountered so far. He was 18, and he was constantly high from the moment I met him, off of something different almost every time. At the time,

I didn't know him well enough yet to know exactly what he was on, but I'd soon learn to deduce what it was according to his behavior.

He was objectively attractive. Everyone could see it, judging by the way every girl tried to butt into our group's conversation, all their eyes fixed on him. But the whole time, he was looking at me. Feeling special was my weakness, and he discovered it quickly.

"You'll be there tonight, right?" he said, looking me up and down.

I nodded. "Sure. I can make some time."

He charmed me. I was 13 and fascinated by his life. Most guys in town that were his age were in college, but he wasn't. Actually, I didn't really know what he did with his time besides getting high. But he just seemed so *cool*. I loved the way he talked, the way he'd have a hand on me at all times, and I didn't shy away from PDA. Our relationship bloomed almost instantly, but then we'd butt heads, and it would stop just as abruptly. The whiplash from the affection and then lack thereof made my head spin and got me addicted.

It was a whirlwind romance, or at least that's what I told myself. We dated on and off–months of closeness, coming to a sudden halt when he decided to break up with me for one reason or another. Sometimes, he'd suddenly decide that I was too young for him after all; other times, it was to "protect" me from him and his lifestyle. I felt protected enough for the most part; despite all the drugs he'd take, he'd never, *ever* let me take any on his watch. He was at his angriest whenever someone offered me coke at a party. He'd whisk me away in a heartbeat, keeping me away from anyone who used as much as he did. "I don't want you to turn out like me," he'd say.

I was more often than not going insane during this period of my life, but I'd be at my craziest whenever we broke up.

We'd go months without seeing each other, and then, after some drunken night with my friends, I'd walk all the way across town at 3am to his place. It took an hour of walking to get to him, and I'd do it carelessly just to show up crying on his doorstep. He'd take me in every time. In a life full of uncertainty, it was nice to be at least sure of him.

My Mom and stepdad would visit Brasília a lot. I thought of it as a sort of forbidden land, the place that my Mom had run away to so many years ago to get away from us. My stepdad had family there, including a younger sister with Down syndrome that he took care of most weekends. I didn't usually go with them, of course. You probably know by now that I had my prejudices against family events in general. But on one particular occasion, Jonas happened to be visiting a friend in Brasília the same weekend.

"Who do you know in Brasília?" my Mom asked me as she packed her bag.

"I know people," I said vaguely, not wanting to tell her about Jonas. "I just want a bit of a weekend getaway. I'll just be with them for the day."

She sighed. "Yeah, okay. I guess…I guess that's fine."

I knew she didn't trust me, but I'd been kissing up to her all week to guarantee I could execute my plan this weekend. Ultimately, she wanted to mend our relationship, and I took advantage of that.

It was my plan all along to stay at Jonas's friend's apartment overnight, but I couldn't say that off the bat. I had to ease her into it. She dropped me off Saturday morning and I was a bundle of nerves. It was the first time I had planned to sleep at a *boy's* house. No, a *man's*, I reminded myself. He was 18, after all.

A guy I didn't recognize opened the door for me. He smiled. "Cris?"

I nodded shyly. "Yeah. Hi."

"I'm Adrian," he said, looking me up and down the same way Jonas did when we first met. I wondered if they all did that. "Come on in."

The apartment was mostly full of other guys around Adrian's and Jonas's age. A handful of girls hung around, everyone older than me, most of them smoking or drinking. I found Jonas in one of the bedrooms in the back, shooting something into his arm. It was the first time I saw him using a needle.

He looked up at me, surprise in his eyes. "Cris, you're here."

He immediately took the needle out of his arm and walked over to me, pulling me into his arms for a hug. He smelled like smoke and a cologne I recognized but didn't know the name of, and a hint of weed. I couldn't see anything when he hugged me–he was so tall and I was tiny next to him, I'd be swallowed whole by his chest every time. I closed my eyes and sunk into him.

The next few hours were a blur. I most often sat on Jonas's lap, his arm around my waist, holding me close to him. There was a bong, and beer, and coke on the table that Jonas wouldn't let me touch. At some point, I felt sober enough to call my Mom and tell her that I was going to stay the night after all. Yes, there were girls there, I said, which was technically true. No, I wouldn't share a bed with a boy, I lied. She agreed to let me stay.

A part of me knew I was going to lose my virginity that night. I wanted it to be Jonas. I didn't care that I wasn't his first as long as he was mine.

He made me feel beautiful. I remember when I was 12 and still living with Madonna when she'd do anything and everything, she could to try to make me uninterested in boys. One day when we were sitting on the front porch, she casually remarked, "It's such a shame. You have beautiful eyes, a beautiful nose, and a beautiful mouth. It's just…the combination of everything on your face that just doesn't go together."

Madonna was a lot of things, and I knew a liar was included in that. *She* wasn't even necessarily pretty. But her attitude caught my Dad's attention in the first place, her candidness and ability to get what she wanted. But my Mom–my Mom was beautiful. It's why all of the women who pined after him knew they never really stood a chance as long as my Mom was around. I wanted to be *that* kind of pretty–the kind of pretty that would make people forget all about my poor reputation. Even prettier than my Mom, if I could.

In comparison, even with all of Jonas's faults and the pushing and pulling of our relationship, I'd take it any day over the turmoil of living at home. At least, here, I knew I was wanted. Or at least, I felt like I was.

CHAPTER 13

And Keep on Spiraling Out of Control

Everything was spiraling out of control, more than I ever thought possible. The intensity of my relationship with Jonas consumed me. I was drunk more often than not, while he was nearly always high. Jonas started using injection drugs more than anything else, and his arms were always spotted with bruises. He was moody and aggressive, and although he'd never physically hurt me, our arguments were worse than ever. Where he'd once made me feel grown up, he now made me feel like a kid. I started to feel looked down upon, a feeling I hated more than almost any other. A part of me started to resent him. And yet, for some reason, I couldn't get enough of him.

On one of our many breaks, I got a call from a number at my Mom's house that I didn't initially recognize. "I'm looking for Cris," the guy on the other end said.

"Who is this?" I asked, unable to place his voice.

"You don't remember?" His voice was flirty, but I still had no idea who he was. "I'm hurt."

"Um, no, I don't remember," I replied honestly. "So, can you tell me who this is before I hang up?"

He laughed. "It's Adrian! You stayed at my place in Brasília a few weeks ago."

"Oh." I vaguely remember a guy with dark hair opening the apartment door for me, maybe offering me a beer or two. From what I remember, he was cute. I'd barely paid attention to him that weekend–I was too focused on Jonas–but I wasn't going to admit that. "Hey. How'd you get my number?"

I could sense him shrugging through the phone. "Looked you up, wasn't too hard. How've you been?"

Terrible, I thought, but I didn't say it. "Um, fine. Same old. How about you?"

"Oof, you don't sound fine." How did he see right through me so quickly? Was I really that transparent? "What's going on?"

I sighed. "Uh, Jonas and I broke up. It's fine."

"Again?" Great, so he knew about our tumultuous history. I wondered how much Jonas had told him. Were these sober conversations that they'd had? Probably not, I assumed. "Aw, man, I'm sorry to hear that."

"Thanks for that."

"But not too sorry."

I paused. Although I picked up on his flirtatious tone earlier, I didn't expect him to be so direct. It caught me off guard. I decided to play dumb. "And why's that?"

"Well, you're pretty," he said. "And you seem fun and nice. Nicer than Jonas, that's for sure."

"I'm not really all that nice."

"Regardless, I think we'd get along. I want to get to know you better."

I knew what that actually meant. "I want to get to know you better," coming from a guy almost always meant, "I want to sleep with you." But I was honestly due for a rebound, and what would be better revenge than meeting up with a friend of Jonas? It was petty, and I knew that, but I wasn't planning on ever actually sleeping with him. Maybe just getting some extra attention to bide my time and get Jonas's attention.

"When are you visiting Brasília again?" he asked.

"Um, my parents are heading over there next weekend."

"Stay at my place." It wasn't a question. I had to admit I was attracted to his decisiveness. It was a luxury I never got with Jonas. "You can sleep over."

"I don't know if my parents would be okay with that." I didn't know why I was making excuses. I was hesitant, even though I'd already made up my mind.

"They were okay with it before."

"Well, that was different. There were people there."

"So just tell them there are gonna be people here. Do you have something against lying?"

"Definitely not."

"Great. So you'll be here." Again, not a question. My heart skipped a beat. "I'll see you next Saturday?"

"Sure."

We talked on the phone nearly every other day for the next two weeks leading up to my visit to Brasília. I'd never answer his calls if my Mom or stepdad were home, nor if there were any friends around. I wanted to keep him like my own special secret. And maybe after I saw him, then I'd consider letting word get out of us meeting up, at least just to get back at Jonas. I wanted to make him a little jealous, and Adrian was an opportunity for that and a chance for the attention I craved, nothing more.

Again, I told my Mom there was a party, except this time, it was a blatant lie. There were loopholes I clung onto last time–the fact that there were, in fact, other people around. And yeah, there were girls, even if I didn't pay attention to them.

Jonas and I might as well have been completely alone. But this time, there was no party to sort of lie about. It was just me and Adrian.

I'd gotten too used to hanging out with older guys, so I wasn't as nervous as I should've been as I walked up to his now-familiar apartment door in the late afternoon. He opened the door before I could even knock, expecting my arrival. "Hey," he said, in his now-familiar voice and his now-somewhat-familiar dark hair and brown eyes and sharp jaw. The lack of softness in his face was striking, but it was somewhat different to Jonas's typical intensity. Jonas was all sunken in, hollow, probably from all the drugs he took. Adrian, on the other hand, looked almost *too* healthy, like he cared a bit too much about appearances. He looked like the type of guy who did jaw exercises to maintain his facial structure, an unnecessary upkeep.

He kissed me hello, and it felt natural even though we'd barely touched before. I wondered if this was due to his directness over the phone that I'd grown accustomed to. He invited me in, offered me a beer, and lit up a cigarette. I took a puff whenever he offered, which wasn't too often. We talked; I don't remember what about. We kissed in between conversation. But this only lasted about an hour or two when there was a loud pound on the door.

I jumped, startled, as Adrian got up and walked towards the door. He was about to put his hand on the doorknob when we heard a voice on the other side: "Cris? Open the door!"

Oh, no. Adrian turned to look at me, and I cringed. "Who is that?" he whispered.

"My Mom," I said apologetically. Ever since my last visit to Brasília, she'd kept an eye on me more than usual. I had a feeling that she suspected something was going on more than my usual shenanigans. I hated that she was right, that she somehow had a motherly instinct even after not being my mother for most of my life. I especially hated that she decided to *show up* here and embarrass me like this before I could even get a really good kiss in.

He shuffled back over to me, keeping his steps quiet and his voice low. "What does she think you're doing here?"

I knew what he was doing–trying to get his story straight. I'd done it one too many times. "A party," I whispered, following his lead.

"Okay, well, obviously, there's no party," he said. "Let's pretend we're not here, okay?"

The knocking on the door continued, switching between doing that and trying the doorknob again and again. Suddenly, the knocking sounded much stronger, and we heard a man's booming voice. "Cris, open this door *right now!*"

Adrian looked at me. "Is that your Dad?"

"Stepdad," I corrected.

"Same thing," he said, and I felt somewhat offended by his brazenness. *Not the same thing at all, but okay.* "Let's go out the back."

"You have a back door?" I asked. "You're…you're on the second floor."

"There's a window."

"A *window?* You want me to *jump?*" I wasn't sure I was that desperate.

He rolled his eyes. "No, no, there's a fire escape we can crawl down."

"Oh." I nodded. The knocking and yelling continued, but it sounded like just my Mom's voice now. "Okay, let's go."

Although I tried to cover it up, I was *mortified.* I came here to feel more grown up, but instead, I felt more childish than ever. What was I even *doing* here? I barely knew Adrian. What if he gossiped about this? He was *definitely* going to tell people about my parents showing up. How *embarrassing*. What would Jonas say when he found out? What if word gets out back in Goiânia, and I gain another reputation as a neighborhood slut, but this time with older guys? And this time, instead of being my Mom's fault, it would be all my fault.

These thoughts raced through my head as we tiptoed as fast as we could to the back window. I was a step behind Adrian, who reached the window before me. He peered outside and then immediately ducked to the ground, pulling my arm along with him, causing me to stumble as I crouched next to him.

"What, what's wrong?" I asked.

"Your *Dad*," he said through gritted teeth, visibly frustrated.

"Stepdad." Not the time, but it was a reflex to correct anyone who referred to him as my Dad.

He ignored me and leaned forward slightly to get another glimpse without exposing himself too much. He scowled. "He's just *standing* there."

I copied his position and took a peek. He really was just standing there, staring at the exact window we were planning to crawl out of. The pavement wasn't too far down from the fire escape, and I honestly believed that he would try to climb up if it weren't for the fact that the ladder was out of reach. He opened his mouth, and I could hear his distant voice yelling, "*Cris?!*" through the windowpane.

"What now?" I asked.

"You got us into this, you don't have any ideas?" he shot back.

I frowned but didn't reply.

He looked at me with a sigh. "Look, he can't stay out there forever. We just have to wait him out."

"But that might take a while," I admitted. "He's...pretty stubborn."

Just to embarrass myself further, he didn't take long waiting around at all. About 5 minutes after I said that he shook his head and went back around the building, probably to meet my Mom at the door again, who was now knocking at briefer intervals.

The moment he rounded the corner, Adrian sprang into action. He pushed open the window and immediately crawled through, not waiting for me to follow, but I did anyway. He opened the ladder, and we shimmied down the fire escape together.

Once we hit the pavement, Adrian kept walking without looking back at me. I felt a sudden pang in my chest, the familiar feeling of being a burden to someone. The entire time I lived with my Dad and Madonna, I felt like a burden to them. It was the same feeling I got that night with Adrian as he walked into an alleyway, weaving between buildings, not checking to see if I was following him because he knew I was. It was getting darker by then; the sun had already set some time ago, and the last rays of light were fading from the sky quickly. The wind blew through my frame, and I wrapped my arms around myself, a bit chilly. I didn't bring a sweater, not expecting to be outside at this time. Adrian had his sweater on, hands in his pockets. He briefly glanced at me, noticed me rubbing my arms to get some heat in them. He didn't offer me his sweater.

He stopped in an alley and lit a cigarette he'd brought with him, leaning against the wall of a brick building. We could see his apartment from here, and we watched the front door, waiting for my parents to come out of it and leave so we could go back inside. He offered me his pack of cigarettes and lighter without looking at me. When we were inside, he'd offer me his own cigarette or light it for me himself. Now, it seemed like he was offering more out of stiff politeness than anything else. Because he felt like he *had* to. I sunk into myself, the burdening feeling returning. I was thirteen, smelling smoke in an alleyway with a boy who didn't love me and offering me cigarettes. I didn't know the truth yet at that age: that a boy who loves you won't offer you cigarettes.

CHAPTER 14

How Things Got so Bad

All the last bits of light had faded from the sky by the time they finally left. I watched as they walked out of the door, heading down the steps towards their car, their voices raised at each other's, my Mom gesturing wildly with her hands as she spoke and my step-dad throwing his arms up in frustration. I hated them in that moment. For showing up unannounced, for ruining what could have been a good night, and for making me feel like more of a burden than I already did. I hated them for everything. I think I hated myself, too.

Adrian and I walked back to his apartment once they drove away, striding up the steps to his place. I waited for the relief to hit me about the whole situation, and my parents finally being gone, but it didn't. I felt the same dread in my chest that came up like bile the moment they knocked on the door. *It's fine*, I reminded myself. *You got away with it*. But a small part of me pushed away as much as possible, wondering if I wanted to get away with it in the first place. Was I getting tired of all this living? Was it even living at all?

We got to the door of his apartment. He unlocked and opened the door, and I began to follow him inside when he stopped and leaned against the doorframe, blocking me.

"I think you should go," he said simply.

72 | Broken by Love: The Story of an Atheist Turned Pastor

I blinked at him, frozen, thinking maybe I didn't hear him right. "What do you mean?"

"I *mean*," he repeated slowly as if I were stupid. Maybe I was. "I think you should *go*."

"But they're gone now," I reminded him of the obvious, as if *he* were stupid. "There's nothing to worry about, it's fine."

I went to move past him into the apartment, but he shifted and blocked me again. I looked up at him, frustrated and a bit scared. Was he really not going to let me in anymore?

"I don't know, Cris, this kind of brought down the whole vibe," he explained. "You're kind of problematic, and I don't want that sort of energy in my apartment. I gotta protect my own, you know?"

"What are you even *talking* about?" I said, baffled. "It was my *parents'* fault, not mine."

"That's literally the whole problem! The fact that your parents are still causing issues for you in the first place."

I didn't reply. I didn't know what to say, because he was right, and I hated that he was right.

He sighed. "You're just too young, Cris."

And there it was. It was probably the same thing that Jonas thought to himself all the time, too. *Just too young*. I felt smaller than ever, more like a kid than ever.

When I still lived with Madonna, she'd go out of her way to ruin any potential crushes I could even *think* of having. She'd tell me terrible things about them, forbid me from leaving the house, and hit me if she suspected at all that I could have feelings for someone. I know she never wanted the best for me, but moments like this with Adrian made me wonder if *this* was why. Did she have a point this whole time?

"Where am I supposed to go?" I asked, my voice smaller than ever. "I don't...I don't have my stepdad's phone number, and I don't have any money for...for a bus or a taxi–"

"Just go home. Look, I honestly don't care anymore," he replied, gesturing down the hall. "Please, just go."

I glanced over my shoulder toward the door of the apartment building. "I-I don't know how to get home."

He sighed, closed his front door, and locked it behind him as if he were suspicious that I would bolt for it at any time. A part of me wanted to. I wanted to run inside and leave him locked out, banging on the door the same way my mother did. But it's not like that would do me any good in the long run. So, when he headed to the exit of the complex, I followed him.

We walked outside the apartment, and he trotted down the steps casually as if he weren't kicking out a thirteen-year-old girl in an unfamiliar *huge* city after sunset. Once we hit the sidewalk, he pointed down the street.

"Just walk straight that way," he said.

I looked off in the distance, where I could see cars speeding by down a busy avenue. "You're kidding, right?"

He shrugged. "You'll find your way home eventually."

I shook my head. "Adrian, I–"

But when I glanced in his direction, he was already climbing the stairs back up to his house. "Are you *serious?!*" I nearly yelled, my anger taking over my fear for a second.

He didn't look back, just raised his arm in a half-wave as he walked inside and shut the door behind him. I heard the lock slide into place and reality set in that I was really, truly, completely alone.

I didn't have any other options. I looked at the road ahead and started walking.

It took me 20 minutes to reach the road. It was further than I thought, and much, much busier. Also, it wasn't a road like I expected. It was an actual highway. Great.

My knees felt wobbly as I looked forward toward the other side. There was no crosswalk, no stoplights or stop signs, just car after car going between 60 to 80 miles an hour.

I glanced back in the direction of Adrian's apartment. What if I just went back and sat on the apartment steps, hoping he'd let me back in or that my parents would show up? *No.* He already made me feel like enough of a kid. I wasn't about to be a sad puppy, a lost little girl, begging on his doorstep.

I turned to the avenue ahead and took a deep breath. I could do this. I *had* to do this. I didn't have a choice anymore. All I knew was that my stepdad's place in Brasília was 30 minutes away by car. I had no idea how far that would be for me to walk. But I had to do it anyway.

I readied myself, positioning myself in a runner's stance as I looked both ways across the first intersection, all the cars going to the right. I could make it halfway across, pause, and then run across the hoard of cars going to the left.

I watched the cars coming from the right and waited for an opening, estimating the seconds it would take for me to run across compared to the seconds it would take for them to reach me. *Not now…not now…okay, now.*

I bolted. I didn't look at the cars or behind me; I just aimed straight ahead for the small empty space on the road separating the lanes. Cars honked, and I knew it was directed at me. A part of me felt apologetic, embarrassed, wondering what they were thinking. *What the hell does she think she's doing?* The worst part was that I didn't have an answer. I didn't know what I was doing anymore, and I wasn't sure I ever knew in the first place.

I made it to the halfway point without an accident. I stopped, bent over with my hands on my knees to catch my breath. I made it this far. I could make it a bit further. I gave myself a few more seconds to catch my breath before readying myself in the same stance I did the first time. I inhaled. Exhaled. Looked to the left. Waited, waited, waited. And then ran.

More cars honking, more adrenaline rushing, more embarrassment in my mind. *Sorry, sorry, sorry.* The fear grew like roots in my gut, like tentacles. I was terrified, but I couldn't let it paralyze me.

I lived in fear through my entire childhood, and I'd let it paralyze me. Or it was more like I didn't know that I had the power to move in the first place. When I was nine, I'd gone to the store to pick something up for Madonna when I bumped into a neighborhood kid that I'd grown up with. I wasn't interested in him, and I had never had been. We were just talking, saying hello. And then my Dad drove by us, down the street, slowly, watching us. He passed us by without a word, but his face made my heart drop to my stomach. My friend didn't notice. I turned and ran home in the middle of his sentence. He was already angry enough if I talked to any boys, but he'd get even angrier when Madonna instigated. She'd tell him he *should* be mad at me, that I was dating *every* boy in town, just to control my life in any way she could. Everything I did, I did out of fear of them. I started living what I described as fearlessly when I left her and moved in with my Mom, but what I knew in my gut to be a different form of fear, one that propelled me forward, even off of a cliff, even in the middle of traffic.

I made it to the other side, my heart threatening to beat out of my chest. I half-smiled to myself, almost wanting a moment to celebrate. *Did I really just survive that? That's kind of cool.* But then the reality of my situation set in, and I remembered that I still had no idea where I was. No phone, no money, no address, and no one. I sighed to myself and looked up to the sky. I wondered for a moment if there was really a God out there. If He could see the situation I was in. If he could send some sort of rescue. Then my imagination started to run wild, could this be like some kind of ROM-COM. I allowed myself to imagine, just for a second, that I was taking a long walk to the love of my life, waiting for me in a warm house with food, light, and love. And then I let the fear back in, and I kept walking.

After walking for about an hour–always going straight, crossing as many busy roads as I had to, and trying to recognize something, anything–I had to walk through a condo. It seemed friendly enough and was much better than the shady street corners I'd just been to. Every silhouette of a man was in the shape of a threat.

I examined the cars in the parking lot, guessing in my mind who they belonged to. It was pretty easy to distinguish between a family car, a just-married-car, and a single-car. Not to mention the rich-young-adult-car. Guessing the owner in terms of age was the easiest way to distinguish between them.

There were kids playing in the streets, which immediately made me breathe a sigh of relief. I felt warmer here, more at ease. I wondered what it would've been like to live in such a close-knit community. Maybe people liked each other here more than they did in my hometown.

I came across a group of kids playing volleyball. I only realized they were probably around my age when I got closer to them. They looked so young, but I must have, too. I was so used to hanging out with guys older than me that I forgot I didn't really look like them. I was a little girl, playing dress up as a college kid.

I walked over to them, rolling my shoulders back and trying to look taller, older, more mature. Hopefully trustworthy. "Hey," I called out once I reached the edge of the court. They all turned to look at me, and I swallowed the lump in my throat. "Do any of you have a phone I could use?"

They hesitated, looking at each other awkwardly to see which of them would volunteer. After a short beat, a boy my age raised a hand and strode toward me. "I got it," he said, more to his friends than to me.

He led me to a short apartment complex stuffed between two other buildings. It felt odd to be alone in an apartment with a boy and not have any other intentions behind it. We were here, and there was nothing more to it.

He led me to his home phone on the wall next to his kitchen counter and handed it to me. "Go ahead," he said.

"I, um…I don't have their number."

He grabbed the yellow pages off the counter and handed it to me. I muttered a mortified "Thank you," and then scoured through it. What was my stepdad's *Mom's* full name? How would I even go about knowing that? And would it be under what I knew my stepdad by or would it be a different family name I didn't know about? There's no way my Mom would be in here either.

I put the book down with a huff, unsuccessful. "Okay, let me try…"

I had no idea what his phone number could be. I'd never call them when they would visit Brasília, and I hadn't had a reason to since I started coming with them. I couldn't remember if he'd even told me it before.

I took a shaky breath as I picked up the phone, my fingers tracing over the numbers. The only option left was to guess. My legs were exhausted and sore. This was all I had left: one lucky guess.

I punched in the numbers, one by one. *Please, please, please.*

The other end started ringing. And for the first time in a long time, I found myself praying. My stepdad's mom answered the phone. My stepdad paid for the taxi once I arrived at his house. I still wasn't sure how I did it exactly, but I somehow managed to get the phone number right on my first try. My only try. It's hard to accept miracles when they happen to you. It's hard to admit that maybe the thing that just happened to you is a once-in-a-lifetime moment never to be repeated again. It's human nature to brush things off, to shrug to ourselves and say, "I bet this has happened to everyone." But, looking back, I can clearly see that this was the first time in my life that I felt the presence of God. It was a miracle, but I was too hurt and too blind to recognize. It would be almost two decades later for me to recognize how God was taking care of me.

CHAPTER 15

Back to Where it All Started

T hanks to all my impulsivity throughout my 13th year, I ended up failing 7th grade and needed to repeat the year. I skipped school a lot, slept in class, and barely studied. I visited Olímpia a year later, and although I hated the life I had there, hindsight made Madonna's abuse not look as bad. I was tired of running all over the place, getting into new friend groups just to leave them and repeat the same cycle again and again.

At the end of the day, children still crave stability. Madonna knew this too well. I don't remember how our conversation went when I visited, but we had another of our usual late nights. By the end of it, I had agreed to move back in.

I went back to my old school. I turned 14. I repeated 7th grade. I felt like I was in a trance. It was the same thing every day. Madonna would keep me up at night, Dad would turn a blind eye, and brother would go out with his friends and leave me behind. I was still ostracized by the town, especially now that everyone knew I'd spent some time away with my Mom. I kept my head down and just tried to survive to make sure I finished the year this time. Through it all, I began to forget why I'd agreed to return in the first place. Sure, I was back to having a stable routine, but stability didn't equal security in

79

this case. I had two parents again, but their relationship wasn't exactly a good example for me.

I spent that year dissociated, never fully there, so I barely remember any of it. Once I finished 7th grade, upon turning 15, I quickly moved back with my Mom. I was beyond the point of caring if it broke my Dad's heart. I needed to take care of my own heart first.

The stakes felt a lot higher this time.

While living with Madonna, she began to tell me over and over again that I was sure to get pregnant at 15. I remembered being 12 years old, still new to the pursuit of crushes–never kissed anyone or even so much as held hands. I'd fantasize about having some epic love story one day, like the ones I'd watch on TV every day after school. Madonna figured this out pretty quickly and read my diary to use it to her advantage. "I know you like this boy," she'd say during our late-night talks. Her goal was always to discourage me from pursuing anything, to "protect me" from becoming the slut she believed me to be, but all this did was make me want to pursue potential romances even further. Sometimes, it felt like I'd do anything, anything at all to be loved.

I was around that same age when I met my new next-door neighbor, who, in my mind, was a total bad boy. He was sixteen, with black hair, and a red motorcycle. I'd see his motorcycle parked by the curb and watch him drive away to whatever adventures were waiting for him that day. I wanted him to take me with him.

Everyone knew about it when he got into an accident. His gorgeous motorcycle was wrecked, and he was hospitalized with severe injuries. There was a good chance he'd never walk again. It must have been devastating for him and his family. But I, being 12 years old and childish and selfish, saw this as an opportunity to get closer to him. It was just like the movies, I thought. A tragic incident brings a meant-to-be couple together. Maybe we were soulmates, and this was the beginning of our story. I wrote all my little daydreams down in my diary; I even charted out a plan. *When he got home from the hospital,* I told myself *I'd feed him in bed. I'll help him with his physical therapy. Maybe I'll even be the reason he walks again.* It was incredibly self-centered of me, I know. But at that age, I really would do anything to love and be loved back.

Of course, Madonna read my diary again. But this time, she was discreet about her invasion of my privacy. Instead of telling me outright that she'd read it like she usually would, she instead started making up rumors about the boy next door.

"Have you seen the line of girls he has out there every day?" she'd say. I actually hadn't seen many girls around. But she thought of her answer for this too. "They go there every morning while you're in school. Carrying food for him, all that. I heard he has *tons* of girlfriends." And then, the final blow: "I wouldn't be surprised if he got one of those fifteen-year-olds pregnant soon."

This turned me off from him entirely, and I immediately stopped my plans to pursue him. It was years later that I realized that she'd once again read my personal thoughts and used them to manipulate me by talking about one of my worst fears.

Years later, the fear still hadn't faded. Now that I was 15, I felt like I was skating on thinner ice than ever before, and it was starting to crack beneath me. I had to prove that I wasn't the slut that everyone thought I was. I wasn't like my Mom. I couldn't be.

When I moved back in with her, she was living in a new building that she managed. I didn't see Willis as much anymore, which I was surprisingly okay with. I wanted a new start, to make all new friends. Even though I was put back into the same school, this seemed like the perfect opportunity to do so.

CHAPTER 16

Another Weekend Alone, Another Party

I found a new group of friends pretty quickly, a huge group of boys at my school. I don't remember exactly how we became acquainted; I think I met one of them, who introduced me to all the rest, about 20 of them. We were inseparable from then on. I'd see other girls come and go in the group–girlfriends, flings, or just new friends who I viewed as wannabe mini-me's. But I was the only consistent girl in their group. Well, that is what I wanted to believe. That was a huge ego booster to be the only girl in such a big group of guys.

They were what I called playboys. Super spoiled with rich parents, expensive cars, big houses, and even bigger parties. They'd go racing often, at least twice a week. I felt special when I tagged along; like they were a team, and I was their cheerleader. I'd normally stay on the sidelines and watch. Whenever I'd sit in the front seat of one of their cars, the driver would refuse to race. "I can't, Cris is here." I'd blush at this, and they knew it. They made me feel special.

Of course, being the only girl in a group of guys means there's bound to be plenty of rumors. To some, not everyone, I was rumored to be a slut in school. I hated it. But at least here, I had that reputation of my own accord, without my mother's history, and I also knew for myself that I wasn't doing anything wrong. I hadn't even kissed any of these boys. From my point of view, it was a completely innocent friendship. But judging from my last experience having guy friends, I should've known better.

I was home alone one weekend while my Mom went to visit my little sister in Olímpia. I used to go with her every time she'd visit, but I quickly realized there was nothing left for me there. I didn't want to see my Dad or Madonna, and my brother still thought me to be a traitor. I loved my sisters but seeing them just hurt us both. What was the point of going back? Just to relive my childhood traumas all over again? No thanks. So once a month, when my Mom left town, I was alone.

On this particular weekend, the boys were having another huge party in one of their parents' penthouse apartments. I hadn't been to this particular place before, and I was excited to see it. I'd heard he had a rooftop pool, so I made sure to wear my cutest swimsuit. Although there was nothing romantic or sexual going on with any of them, I still enjoyed attention from anyone. Maybe that's why, after everything, I felt like it was my fault.

There were about 50 people at the party. It went on for hours. I considered myself to be a pretty extroverted person, but it proved to be too much even for me. After a couple of drinks and a swim in the pool, I stumbled upon a TV room where I decided to take a break. The apartment was so big it felt more like a mansion. There was room after room after room. I wondered what they used all of them for.

The host of the party, Christian, found me there about an hour later. "Tired?" he asked me.

I nodded, glancing at him quickly before turning my eyes back to the TV. A channel was playing the entire season of a show, and I'd been watching since episode 3. I was on episode

84 | Broken by Love: The Story of an Atheist Turned Pastor

7 now, and I didn't want to miss any of it. "Yeah. It's just a lot sometimes, you know?"

He sighed. "Yeah, you don't need to tell me. I throw these things all the time, and I get so drained." He plopped down on the couch next to me. "Can I lay on you?"

"Sure," I said, not thinking twice about it. The guys would often lean on me, and I on them. There was nothing weird about it to me.

He rested his head on my lap and watched the show with me. "Oh, I've seen this, I think. Doesn't he–"

I shushed him. "No spoilers! I haven't seen this before."

"Oh, my bad. It's pretty good, though."

I didn't say anything. I don't know how long we watched for, but it was long enough to finish the season. My eyes felt heavy by the time it ended. He sat up, moving his head off me for the first time in hours, and I noticed that my left leg had fallen asleep. I shook it, trying to wake it up.

Christian stood and walked over to the door, peering out. I followed, realizing for the first time how quiet it'd gotten out there. The music had stopped, and I didn't know how long it had been off for. When we stepped outside, we realized there were only a few stragglers still there, and everyone else had left.

"What time is it?" I asked, my voice hoarse.

"A lot later than I thought." He laughed. The remaining few boys, friends from the same group we were in, came up to us to say good night before they headed out.

"I probably need to go too," I said.

"Cris, you look exhausted," one of our friends said. "Can you walk home alright?"

"Yeah, I don't live far." I touched the pockets of my shorts then, feeling for my wallet where I kept my house key. It wasn't there. My eyes widened. "Oh no, I think I dropped my wallet somewhere. Have you guys seen it?"

"Why do you need your wallet now?" another boy asked.

"It has my house key in it." I groaned. "How am I gonna get inside? It's not like there's a window I can sneak into."

"Your Mom isn't even home, right?" Christian asked. "Why don't you stay here? Since she's not around anyway. There are lots of empty rooms, you could crash in one."

"Are you sure?" I asked, more concerned about intruding on his space than anything else. I didn't think to be cautious for any other reason.

"Yeah, absolutely. My parents don't get back until Monday." It was Saturday.

"Mine too," I said, and then shrugged. "Yeah, okay, I'll stay if you really don't mind. I'm so tired."

Christian told me he didn't mind. We walked our friends to the door said good night. He led me upstairs, where there was an empty guest room with a bathroom attached to it. He gave me a towel and told me to freshen up. I thanked him profusely. He acted like a total gentleman.

In the end, I still don't know if he was the one who took my wallet. I never found it again.

CHAPTER 17

Me Too

After taking a quick shower to wash the remaining chlorine off of me, I hopped into the guest bed and curled under the blankets. I was exhausted after such a long party and so ready to finally get some rest. I closed my eyes and waited for sleep to wash over me.

The door creaked. I thought I'd closed it. I opened my eyes to see Christian's silhouette in the doorway. All the lights in the apartment were off. I thought he was just checking on me before going to bed himself. But then he entered the room and closed the door behind it. And locked it. I watched, confused, and squinted in the darkness to see him slip the key into his pocket. "Christian?" I said groggily.

He came over to the bed silently. My eyes followed him. Instead of sitting on the side of the bed like I thought he would, he pushed back the blankets that covered me and laid on top of me, resting his full weight on me. "Christian?"

He began to move, and my eyes widened as I suddenly realized what he was trying to do. I was fully awake now, a burst of energy rushing through me. I tried to push him off timidly, but he was too heavy. "Christian, what are you doing?"

"Just stay here," he said, his voice low. His hands reached down.

I pushed him more aggressively, and he budged a bit, giving me enough room to scramble back and sit up, scooting away from him. My eyes were fully adjusted to the darkness now, and I could see his face better. It was completely neutral. "What–what are you doing?" I asked again, even though I knew exactly what he was doing.

"Cris, come on, don't play dumb," he said casually, leaning towards me. I leaned back, away from him, as much as I could. My back was pressed against the headboard. "You stayed over for a reason."

"Yeah, because I'm *tired* and lost my *key.*" It was then that I began to wonder if he was the one who'd taken it. He was laying on my lap for hours, and I was so invested in the show that he definitely could've taken it without me noticing. I shook it off, deciding to focus on the problem at hand. "Christian, I wasn't...trying to imply anything."

"Well, I was." He scooted closer to me. I looked around for an escape route. How could I get out of this without messing up our friendship? And my friendship with all the other guys? They all loved Christian, and who knew what Christian would say about me once this was over? "I mean, you came over while your Mom's gone. We were laying together for *hours–*"

"*You* joined *me,*" I insisted. "*You* laid on *me.* And *you* invited me over. I didn't initiate any of this!"

"But you agreed," he said. "So you clearly wanted it, too."

"*What?*" I was astonished. How had I ever given that impression? I barely even looked at him when he joined me in the TV room. Regardless, this wasn't the time to shoot his ego down. I didn't mind taking responsibility for this as long as it got me out of there. He put his hand on my thigh and began to slide it up. I moved it away, pulling my knees to my chest and wrapping my arms around them. "Look, I'm–I'm sorry if that's the impression I gave, but it really wasn't my intention–"

He leaned in and kissed me then, his mouth open. I instinctively jumped back off the bed. I internally cringed. That was definitely going to offend him, which would make him want to say terrible things about me to our friends. I had to find a way out of this without messing anything up. I felt like I was defusing a ticking bomb and every wrong move I made just quickened the countdown to detonation.

"Christian, I'm sorry, but this can't happen," I said, trying to sound regretful but firm at the same time. "You're my friend. We're *friends*."

He stood and approached me, grabbing my wrists at my sides and leaning in to kiss me again. I turned my face, and his lips met my cheek. I hated the way it felt.

He stayed close to me as he spoke. "You're not friends with anyone," he said. "You're just *easy*. That's why you hang out with us."

This both hurt and confused me. Easy? I hadn't so much as kissed any of them. Did they all think this of me? Did they all assume that I was sleeping with every guy except them?

I ran over to the door and tried turning the knob, just in case. It wouldn't budge.

"That door is staying locked," he said, approaching me again, "until you give in. And I know you will. A part of you wants this, too."

"I-I don't," I stammered. "I didn't–I didn't mean to make you think that."

"Cris, come on, you *know* what you're doing. Stop playing hard to get."

Why was he so determined? I felt more frustrated than afraid of his actions. Couldn't he take a hint? I straightened my posture, deciding to be firmer.

"Christian. I *don't* want to do this. Can you just—can I just go to sleep, please? I'm really tired. And I *don't want this.*"

"You're lying," he insisted. "Things don't have to be this hard, can you stop being dramatic?"

He wasn't going to give in. I could see that now. I examined his body in the dark. He was bigger than me, taller, and visibly stronger, too. I could see the muscles on his arms his chest. The fear finally began to settle in, seeping through the frustration. He was still walking towards me, but he was far enough away for me to think of what to do. I glanced toward the bathroom, the door still open, wondering if I could make it before he got too close. It was about 5 big steps away. *The longer I think about it, the closer he's going to get.* I bolted.

My heart felt like it was going to explode out of my chest in those 5 steps. I could hear his footsteps behind me and feel the distance between us. I made it inside and slammed the door, bolting it as he threw his weight against it. He tried the doorknob, jiggling it, and then began pounding. "Cris, come on, get out of there. This is stupid."

I didn't respond. I looked around, seeing if there was any way out, but of course there wasn't. I was trapped. But it felt better than being in the room with him. He kept switching between trying the doorknob and hitting the door, over and over, telling me to come out. He never yelled; he never cursed at me. It was a weird thing how his tone felt less aggressive than his actions.

I turned the bathroom light on and sat on the floor, my back against the wall. I leaned my head back and closed my eyes. I was *so tired.* I just wanted to sleep. But Christian had to tire out eventually, right? Whenever he calmed down or fell asleep, I could get out of there. Or maybe someone would come home and interrupt, giving me a chance to escape. He couldn't keep me here forever.

Minutes went by. And then hours. He'd mostly stopped banging on the door but would periodically try the doorknob again and groan, "Cris, come on." I stayed there, sitting on the floor the whole time, unresponsive. I felt like one of those prisoners in movies who'd tally their locked-up days on the wall.

Finally, Christian was quiet for a longer period of time. About 30 minutes. I'd been in the bathroom for two hours by then. Maybe he'd fallen asleep. Or at least calmed down enough to talk. I got to my feet and took a deep breath before slowly pushing open the door.

It was light out now. I knew it was Sunday morning, but I had no idea what time it was. I just wanted to get home and finally sleep. I peered out, scanning the room for Christian. He was lying in bed, eyes closed, breathing softly. *Please let him be asleep,* I thought to myself.

I pushed the door open further, cringing when it creaked, and tiptoed out towards the door. I put my hand on the doorknob and tried to turn it. *Still locked.* I'd completely forgotten. I turned around to look at Christian on the bed. Was the key still in his pocket? Could I get it out without waking him?

I hesitated but quickly realized I didn't have a choice. It's not like I could jump out the window of the top floor of an apartment building. I snuck over as quietly as I could and looked around the drawers just in case he'd taken it out of his pocket. It was a long shot; I knew it was, but I had to try. Of course, it wasn't there. *How was I going to do this?*

I turned around to head towards him and try to fish the stupid key out of his pocket, hoping he was in a deep enough sleep, but I stopped in my tracks when I saw that he wasn't asleep at all. He was staring right at me, sitting up in bed. The fear began to settle in me again.

"Christian," I choked out. "Hey, I'm…I'm really tired, and my Mom is gonna be home soon." It was a lie, but I hoped he didn't know that. I couldn't remember if I'd previously mentioned when she was gonna be getting back. "Can you open the door?"

He didn't speak as he pushed himself out of bed and walked over to me. He still didn't say anything as he put his hand on my shoulder and put his lips to mine again. This time, I let him. Maybe if I just kissed him, he'd be satisfied enough to let me leave. Maybe this was a goodbye kiss. Maybe this wouldn't go any further.

He began to push me back toward the wall, and my heart sank to my stomach. *No, no, no.* I broke away from the kiss as I made contact with the wall behind me. I was cornered. "Christian, can I leave, please?"

He moved his hands to my waist and tried to kiss me again. I dodged. "I told you already. You're not going anywhere."

I felt a surge of adrenaline as I decided that I needed to take more drastic measures. I shoved him, and he stumbled back, caught off guard. *What now?* The door was still locked; what was pushing him gonna do except piss him off? But maybe if I fought him off for long enough, he'd tire out and let me go. I braced myself, preparing to fight him as much as I needed to.

He lunged for me and knocked me over, causing us both to fall into the wall where a sharp corner dug into my back. I groaned in pain, and either Christian didn't hear or didn't care because he tried to crawl on top of me again, pushing my back even further into the corner. I began to hit his back, yelling at him to stop, but he stayed on top of me and fumbled with the button on my pants. The corner dug deeper and deeper into me, and I felt like it was going to split me open. I imagined the bright red gash it could leave, a deep cut, and all the questions my Mom would ask as a result of it as he pushed me more and *more and more.*

"Fine!" I yelled. "Fine, just *stop!* Stop, and I'll do it!"

He stopped pushing. He relaxed and retracted some of his weight, and I was met with instant relief from the pain. I took deep breaths, calming myself before I met his eye. He was watching me expectantly.

"Fine," I said again. "Let's just...get this over with."

He cracked a smile for the first time all night as his hands reached for me again.

He fell asleep right after. The door stayed locked until he woke up. Finally, I walked home. I never spoke to any of the boys in that group again. But I didn't cry. I didn't know yet exactly what I'd lost. I just blamed myself, feeling like I'd instigated the whole thing. Maybe he was right–I shouldn't be hanging out with so many guys all the time. Of course, they'd think I'm easy. Of course, this would end up coming of it. *Of course.*

Rumors spread quickly. It didn't take long for all the boys to know we'd slept together. I was mortified and wanted to explain that I didn't have any other choice but thought that might just embarrass me even more.

So, I stayed silent. No one ever knew a thing.

CHAPTER 18

Not the ROM-COM Happy Ending I Wished For

My relationship with my Dad and brother just got even rockier the more time I spent away from them. For most of my 15th year, when my Mom would invite me to go with her to visit them, I'd refuse. But after everything that had happened with Christian, I wanted a change of scenery. So the next month, when she invited me to go with her, I went.

I feigned excitement to see my family. Truthfully, I didn't care how they felt about me as much as I used to. It seemed like my reputation was solidified before I was even born, to friends and family alike. What did it matter anymore?

I mostly avoided their house that weekend. I knew where to go on Saturday night–the food trucks in the town square, like I used to every weekend when I lived there. I knew I'd see some familiar faces, and although I knew most of them didn't like me, I was fine with receiving fake niceties for the night. At 15, I looked much prettier than I had when I was 12 or 13 or even just the year before. A lot had changed in every way including my looks. Because I was better looking now, I knew I'd receive better treatment from the girls and guys alike. This was a sad truth, but I was fine with pretending we liked each other. I sat with a group of girls under the string of lights that stretched across the food trucks, talking and laughing when nothing was really funny. It felt nostalgic, in a way, like I was reminiscing on a life that was never really mine. But I'd always wanted it to be mine so badly. I was getting a taste of the way I wanted to be treated in my childhood, and I wasn't about to let that go to waste.

We watched the rich boys driving their nice cars around the food trucks. To them, this was like a car show. They'd honk their horns or blast music from their radios, cat-calling the girls at the tables and inviting us for a ride. Most of the time, these guys had girlfriends in the next town over and would come to Olímpia for a quick make-out session. Because of this, most girls would giggle and flirt a bit but ultimately say no, and the ones who hopped in the backseat were considered to be easy. It was a weird double standard–the boys were the ones begging for our attention, but if we were to give too much of it at any point, we'd be immediately ostracized.

Still, we'd feel flattered when their headlights shone on us. When they called us by name, we'd blush and fake humility because it's what we were supposed to do. But honestly, I was really, *really* tired of doing what I was supposed to do.

A new truck joined the lineup, playing a song I vaguely knew. There were two boys in the car itself, one driving and one in the passenger's seat, but a gaggle of about seven boys sat or stood in the long bed of the truck. The girls and I watched them, curious as to who these newcomers might be. It was difficult to see them in the dark. Then they passed under some streetlights and I felt a flash of recognition for one of them. He was standing, leaning against the rear panel, scanning the groups at tables. Our eyes met, and I could see the recognition on his face, too.

Massimo.

I hadn't seen him since I was 13. In the one year I came back, I isolated myself and didn't see any of my old friends. He looked different now–taller, tanner, his blonde hair and blue eyes were as beautiful as ever. My heart thumped faster in my chest, so loud that I thought he might hear it.

He cupped his hands around his mouth as the truck made a loop. *"Cris!"*

I grinned, unable to help it. His flattery was different than the usual hollering. It was from Massimo. *My* Massimo.

He beckoned me with his hand. I could feel the girls' eyes on me at the table, and I glanced at them for a moment. They were giggling, teasing me. I could tell they didn't believe I would actually go, and for a moment, I appreciated this change of pace. When I was a child, my reputation was that I'd end up just like my mother and that I'd go with any boy that came along. In my time away from here, that had changed somewhat. Maybe they'd forgotten about all the nasty rumors, or maybe they were trying to give me the benefit of the doubt.

I almost felt sorry, that their newfound belief in me was going to waste. But not sorry enough to stay.

I got to my feet and bolted to the truck, still making its rounds. Two other girls had already climbed on. I chased after them, and the truck slowed down. Massimo extended his hand to me, and I took it with glee.

He boosted me up, and I landed on my feet in the truck bed. We were standing so close, our hands still holding each other, nearly chest to chest. I realized then exactly how tall he'd gotten–I had to look up at him for the first time in my life. I felt breathless.

He smiled at me widely. "Hi," he said. The music from the pickup truck was still blasting and the teenagers around us were screaming, but all I could hear was his voice and his breathing.

"Hi," I said, smiling just as widely.

I looked out towards the horizon at the dim town lights below us. After making a few more rounds, the driver of the truck decided to take us to the local lookout point, the only other Saturday night hotspot. It wasn't too far up; we could see the town square from here, just barely make out all the girls at the tables and the latest rich boys coming in to do their usual loop around the food trucks.

Massimo and I were the only two still sitting in the bed of the truck. Everyone else had hopped off to go drink, smoke, or make out. We stayed there, each with a beer in hand, just talking.

"You got hotter," he said after taking a swig.

I blushed, taken aback. Did he mean it? He wasn't drunk, I could see it in his face. His bright blue eyes were clear, but there was something about them that seemed off. "Yeah, well. Lots of time to work on myself away from here."

"You know, I liked you since we were kids," he said. "I know you know that, but...I don't know, I guess I'm just putting it out there."

"Remember when we used to play house?" I asked. "The whole husband and wife thing. That was so silly. We knew we liked each other; everyone knew."

He looked me up and down. "Never too late to act on it."

My shoulders slumped. I knew what he was implying. I wasn't sure if it was the type of conversation I had imagined myself having with him all this time. I wanted us to catch up, to talk and laugh like old friends did. Yeah, I wanted to kiss him, but where was the build-up to the big moment? Where was the romance? Where was the grand gesture? He only resembled his childhood self in terms of looks, and even then, it was vaguely. It didn't feel like the same kind-hearted kid I remembered him to be.

When we were little, there was a neighborhood Doberman that our friend group was absolutely terrified of. It was always locked up by the fenced yard that we would pass by and tease him. But one time, he escaped and chased after me, barking and snapping its jaws at my feet. I ran for my life until I made it to that big tree in my front yard and reached for a branch to start climbing up, but I wasn't fast enough; it was right behind me, I knew it was going to get me. Suddenly, Massimo jumped in the way and stood between the dog and me. The dog stopped, confused for a moment, but then began growling at Massimo. Massimo looked over his shoulder at me and smiled before he started running, leading the dog away from me.

We looked out for each other back then. He saved me from the Doberman, and when he fell off his bike later that week, I rushed to his side with a tiny first-aid kit I'd dipped into Madonna's cookie jar to buy, specifically for a situation such as this. I'd wanted him to think of me as prepared, womanly, future-wife-material. I wanted that childhood-friends-to-married type of romance.

There was another boy on our block, Dino, who was also known to have a crush on me. He and Massimo would have races down the street on their bikes, and whoever popped the most wheelies would be declared the winner. They'd compete for my attention, but it was never a real competition in my eyes. I barely ever looked at Dino–it was always Massimo for me.

Even at that moment, years later. Even when his eyes didn't quite shine the same way. He was, after all, still Massimo. And there was a lot of history behind that.

And so, despite my disappointment when he leaned in to kiss me, I let him.

I padded down the stairs of my Dad's house the next morning, still groggy from staying out so late the night before. I went to the kitchen to grab a quick breakfast before packing my things to go back to my Mom's place, but I stopped in my tracks when I saw my Dad. I didn't expect to see him there; he was almost always in the store. Or at least, when *I* lived here, he was always in the store. I forgot that some things could change. Who knew? Maybe he hung out in the kitchen more often now.

In reality, he was just looking to corner me. "Where were you last night?"

I shrugged, feigning nonchalance. "Downtown, at the food trucks."

"Were you there all night?"

I nodded.

He sighed. "Cris. The whole town saw you get into the back of a boy's truck."

Oh no. I tried to keep it cool. "It wasn't *just* boys. It was a couple of old friends."

"You know what people think of you here," he said. "Why did you have to make things worse?"

"I'm sorry," I said, and I almost meant it. "I didn't mean to."

"You need to think about these things more," he went on, ignoring my apology. "Honestly, Cris. It's clear to me who's raising you now. I told you what would happen to you if you moved in with your Mom."

I nodded again but didn't reply. I decided I wasn't hungry anymore and turned around, heading back up the stairs to pack.

I felt my cheeks warm with embarrassment. I didn't want to feel embarrassed–I wished I didn't have any regrets about the night before, but I felt like the romantic fantasies I'd had my entire life had just been torn to shreds. Massimo was *far* from gentlemanly. He didn't pressure me to do anything, but I could tell by the way he looked at me that he just wanted someone, anyone, to kiss for the night. It didn't matter if it was me or not, as long as he got it done.

I'd seen many boys look at me that way, and I was sick of it. I wanted someone to look at me with pure adoration. With *love*.

While kissing Massimo, I remembered that most of these rich boys have an out-of-town girlfriend. I pulled away from him and cocked my head, thinking.

"What?" he asked.

"Do you have a girlfriend?" I blurted. I shouldn't have said anything, but I had to know. Massimo was an objectively handsome guy; it was more than likely that he had a girlfriend.

He shrugged and looked away from me, and I knew I had my answer. "Nothing like that," he said coolly.

I didn't ask any more questions. I didn't need to. I knew with certainty that he was here just for a quick make out, and I was his side chick of the night. All those years spent yearning for Massimo had led to that moment, right there, and fell apart.

I left soon after. He kissed me again, but it didn't feel the same. I felt guilt rotting in my stomach at some poor girl in the next town over who was probably wondering what her boyfriend was doing that night. And I just felt pure disappointment. Disillusionment. If Massimo didn't care about me anymore, then who would?

CHAPTER 19

Is He the One?

I made and lost a lot of friends while living with my Mom. But there's always one that I held onto a little longer, as everyone does. We all have our favorites; and when Leander introduced me to his friends, I found mine.

I was 15 years old in 8th grade. I wasn't sure how I felt about that, but there also wasn't anything I could do about it. I was used to hanging out with people older than me, so it felt strange to be in a classroom full of kids who were younger than me.

I got a job at a movie rental place, just to have something to pass the time, but also to be around more people my age. There was this friend group that would regularly come in, a lot of them would walk in joined at the hip, renting movies from me and laughing at inside jokes with one another. I craved the intimacy they had, but I tried not to show it, shoving down my desperation.

A boy came up to me, holding cash in one hand and a popular comedy film in the other. I recognized him.

"Haven't you seen that already?" I asked.

He let out a small laugh, amused at my knowledge, and although I'd seen him before, I examined him for the first time. His half-smirk, his light hair, tan skin. "Okay. You're either a good worker or an even better stalker," he joked.

I shrugged, unsure as to whether or not I should return his banter. I often forgot how to interact with people well, and this was one of those times. I settled for taking his money, counting it up, and collecting his change to deposit in his hand.

He inched his hand forward as I dropped off his change, and there was more skin contact than I expected than there should have been.

"Why don't you join us?" he asked me, and when I looked up to meet his eyes, they were genuine. He nodded his head toward his friend group. "Plenty of room. We're watching a pretty good movie."

I glanced at a clock on the wall. "I get off in 30 minutes."

His smile turned to a grin. "Perfect. I can wait."

I opened my mouth to reply when another boy appeared, swinging his arm around the first boy's shoulder. He was all long hair and cheekbones and limbs for miles. "Can I rent something now? You're taking *forever*."

"I'm just talking to a friend!" the first one said defensively. "Aleks, this is…"

He gestured to me, waiting for my reply.

"Cris," I said shyly, clearing my throat when my voice cracked slightly. "I'm Cris."

"Cris," he repeated. "Meet Aleks."

Aleks reached his hand out to me, removing it from around the first boy's shoulders. His hand was big and warmer, and his fingers brushed against my wrist as my fingers wrapped around his hand.

"Good to meet you, Cris," he said, his eyes boring into mine. I couldn't look away. "And did my friend here even tell you his name?"

"Oh, yeah, of course." I looked at the first one, and I noticed was significantly shorter than Aleks. "Yeah, that's kinda important. Sorry. I'm Leander."

"Who doesn't think when he talks to pretty girls," Aleks chimes in. "I know better than him, though."

Leander shouldered Aleks, staking his territory. He cleared his throat. "Anyway, um. Come join us when you're done."

I nodded. "Yeah. Sure thing."

Leander smiled. He turned to leave, Aleks along with him.

"Wait!" I called out.

They both turned, expectant.

"Um…your movie." He'd left it on the counter. It felt like a lame thing to say, but I had to do my job.

Leander cringed to himself. "Yeah, I, um, I guess that's probably important, too," he said, obviously mortified.

Aleks laughed out loud, throwing his head back. "Man, you *really* don't think around pretty girls."

I'd had friends before. Sort of, I guess. But not like this.

Leander and I started dating shortly after. I wasn't in love with him, but I liked him enough. When we'd first met, I thought that he seemed kind. But as we got to know each other, I started to see how ignorant he was, how blinded by his privilege. At times, he even came off as obnoxious. There were always clues along the way, a breadcrumb trail, that always told me we weren't supposed to be together.

He was ambitious and determined. I didn't mind that necessarily–but I'd always been a dreamer, with all the non-existent relationships I'd fantasize about–but it was always in a way that I couldn't bring myself to relate to. He wanted to be a doctor. Pass all his exams, graduate, and go to a nice school. But I just wanted to get by. It was difficult to imagine my future anymore, let alone what my next week would look like. So when he talked to me about doctors and families, all I could do was try to smile and nod along.

My own insecurities didn't help this case either. He clearly viewed himself highly, genuinely believing that he could achieve all these things he intended to pursue. I believed him, too. But I didn't believe in myself. It was hard to shake everything Madonna had always told me, hard to push away the way my Mom looked at me after the way I'd lived so far, the way I still acted in my day-to-day life. Madonna said that I was guaranteed to be pregnant at 15. I was nearly 16 now and more afraid than ever that she'd turn out to be right.

So, with all this, I can't say that I was surprised when Leander broke up with me after two months, right after I'd just gotten fired from my job. I wasn't a good worker, and I wasn't a good girlfriend, so I understood somewhat.

"I'm in love with someone else," he told me, and being the hopeless romantic I always was, I didn't fight it. "I just need someone who's more…on my level, you know? Who has the same aspirations, the same motivation. And I'm sorry, we can be friends, but…I just don't think you're there yet."

Funnily enough, I'm pretty sure my job fired me for the same reasons. Aside from being in love with someone else, that is.

But I wasn't going to let Leander scare me away from the only friends I'd ever had, that I felt comfortable with for the first time in my life. It felt rare, special, like the universe had accidentally given me this extraordinary group of individuals. I couldn't believe that it was all really mine, not yet at least. Good things had a habit of getting away from me.

Lud was one of those good things. She was another girl in our friend group, around my age, and beautiful inside and out. Dark skin and hair, tightly coiled, and a radiant smile whenever she felt happy enough to show it. I hadn't opened up to anyone about everything that had happened to me, about my family and the back-and-forth of it, the tumultuous teen hood I'd been through thus far. But Lud made it all feel okay like the worst of it had passed.

She'd had her own demons—adopted by a white family that she never fully fit in, a constant outsider—and we found ourselves relating on levels that no one else had been capable of in our lives so far. The odds were stacked against us, and neither of us had the best coping mechanisms, but we had each other.

So, when Leander broke up with me, I knew she'd be there for me. I didn't know that Aleks would be, too.

I didn't cry when Leander broke up with me, but I let Lud comfort me anyway. We were at another gathering with everyone outside at a plaza; about thirty people there in total. We sat on top of the table, our feet resting on the seat, watching everyone move around us. Leander was talking in a group of people, his arm around his new girlfriend. She was pretty and well-kept, her hair down and her smile carefree. I wasn't sure I'd ever smiled like that before. She looked happy. They both did.

Lud had known him a lot longer than I had and knew more about his mentality on these things. "If you want my honest opinion on him, he's a lot more prejudiced than he'd care to admit. Makes sense he'd go with someone like her." She shrugged, nonchalant. We both knew breakups happen all the time. "Don't take it personally. What he said to you."

I nodded. I couldn't take it personally if I tried. He only said what I'd already heard my whole life, so it didn't matter much coming from a guy I'd only really known for two months.

"You okay?"

Lud and I looked up to see Aleks sauntering over to join us at the table we'd claimed. I recalled the smile on Leander's girlfriend's face and tried it out. It felt out of place like a puzzle piece squeezed into its wrong spot. "Yeah, we're good," I said.

Lud put her hand on my leg and muttered quickly that she was going to join a group. I nodded, and my head turned to Aleks as she walked away.

Aleks's eyes searched my face. And I knew then that, somehow, he saw right through me.

He sat down on the seat of the picnic bench right next to my feet, his shoulder leaning against my calves. I could feel his warmth through his jacket, through my jeans. We both knew it was the start of something. We just weren't sure what.

Aleks put his hands on my face, cupping it as he kissed me, and I thought, *Okay, so. I guess this is what we were starting.*

I don't remember exactly how it first started happening, but it happened regardless. The kissing became routine, a part of my week I could always look forward to, butterflies rising in my stomach whenever I thought about seeing him again. It wasn't on purpose, but I also think it was inevitable. The moment he first came up behind Leander at that concession stand in the movie theater, when his eyes bore into mine, and our hands touched. I honestly didn't know why I'd bothered with Leander in the first place. I always knew it was going to end up being Aleks.

He was different than the other boys I'd been with right off the bat. In his personality and character—he was the perfect balance between being soft and tough at the same time—but also just in how it *felt* with him. We were so young, just fifteen and seventeen years old, and we both admitted that neither of us had ever really felt that way before.

"Cris, you know me, I'm not the 'settling down' type of guy," he said, using air quotes around "settling down" one night as we lounged in his room while he was home alone.

"But I like this. Just...try to be open-minded about it. We don't want to chain ourselves down, you know? We gotta be freer."

Free. Sure. I could do that.

So, we dated. And for about two months, it was bliss. Being fifteen and in some sort of love–and regardless of what people may say about teenagers, I know we were in love–is always an intense feeling. You're not fully developed in both brain and body, your hormones are going crazy, and everything feels like the end of the world all the time. I felt like I loved Aleks so much that I'd explode at the sheer thought of it, and for once, unlike all the other boys in my past, I knew he felt the same about me. I could feel it in the way he cupped my face, see it in the way he looked at me like he always knew what I was thinking. And the craziest part was that most of the time, he really did know. We were connected somehow, on a level that both of us were still too young to understand.

But (and there's always a but) there was something about that two-month mark that just always made everything fall apart.

"Hey, I'm going to Oktoberfest," I told him, trying to keep my tone casual. "I've been planning this for, like, a while. With some of my friends."

He nodded, his eyes on the book in his hand that he was skimming through, another day in his bedroom. It became more familiar to me with each passing day now–the sole desk in his room, the blankets on pillows on the floor for lack of a mattress, a conscious decision he decided to make during a hippie phase that he felt loyal to. Sprawled out drawings across his desk, *good* ones, too. It suited him.

I was nervous to mention Oktoberfest. Everyone knew what it was for–drinking, partying, and, most of all, making out–and I'd paid for my trip before we started dating. I wasn't about to let that money go to waste, and besides, I *wanted* to go. I wanted a fun weekend with strangers, forgetting all of my problems and maybe even leaving Aleks behind for a little while. Don't get me wrong, I loved him. I knew I did. But I didn't know how to be in a consistent, committed relationship. I felt restless in it, like there was an itch I couldn't scratch, waiting for the other shoe to drop at any moment. The part in the movie when things are too good to be true right before they go bad. I just *knew* I was reaching that point.

Aleks didn't know how to be in a relationship either. He wasn't worried about his reputation for nothing; everyone knew he was a bit of a player and could never keep a girlfriend without cheating on her. I didn't judge him for it because I knew we were in the same boat.

"Yeah, that's fine," he said, not looking up from his book at first. "You'll have fun, you should go."

I nodded in return. "Okay. Cool."

"You know what?" He shut his book and turned to me. I glanced at the cover but didn't recognize it. I thought it was something for school. Was he just reading for fun? I didn't know he did that. "It could be fun for both of us. Let's make it a challenge. See how many people we can pull over the weekend."

I blinked at him. "What?"

"Yeah. We could both see, like, how many people we both kiss over the weekend. You at your festival, and me, just... here." He chuckled like he knew he'd beat me even though I had the advantage.

"Are you...sure you're okay with that?" I wasn't sure how I felt about it, and although Aleks always talked big, I felt like he was pushing it. Both himself and our relationship.

"Why not?" He shrugged, seeming cool as ever, and then sighed and shifted his body further towards me, sensing my doubt. "Remember I told you I don't really settle down? Well,

I wanna settle with you in our own way, I guess. I want you in my life, but I don't want to be…" He paused, searching for the word, his eyes scanning the room and then landing back on me once it came to him. "Tied down. You know? I'm only seventeen, and I want the *freedom*. But I still want you, too. I want both. Maybe this is our way of having both. Does that make sense?"

And looking back, it didn't. I know it didn't. But I wanted it to. So I shrugged back at him, seeing if his coolness could rub off on me. "Okay," I said. "You're right, it could be fun."

He smiled at me and held out his hand to shake, to seal the deal. I took it.

CHAPTER 20

The Oktoberfest Affair

Oktoberfest was fine. Literally just fine. It was fun to be with other friends, a quick getaway from reality, and a couple of days spent without sobering up even for a second, but I did miss Aleks. More than I could bring myself to admit with him. And with every guy I kissed came the guilt gnawing at me, clawing its way up my throat, threatening to spill through my lips whenever they touched someone else's.

But he wanted freedom, right? Fine. I'll give him freedom. He wanted a cool, chill girlfriend who was okay with an open relationship? Sure. He wanted to pretend he didn't care? I'd pretend I cared even less. I was determined to beat him at his own game, even if my stomach was in knots every time I tried to sleep at night.

When I got back to town, I proudly told him I'd kissed a total of six guys over my week out of town. I knew I'd made a mistake the moment the words spilled out of my mouth, and his jaw clenched in response. Aleks would always say, "You *know* me, Cris," and he was right. I did. Better than he knew himself. I knew that if I took him up on his little bet, it'd eat him up inside. He couldn't take what he dished out, and I knew it from the moment I laid eyes on him in the movie store. I just wanted to believe differently despite knowing better.

109

That was the first time he broke up with me. Although we'd dated the same amount of time that Leander and I had dated, just two short months, I was *wrecked.*

It wasn't the same as Leander. Lud knew that. Leander was way more of a jerk than Aleks was, and although Leander had introduced me to the friend group first, Aleks was the one who made it feel like home. With Leander, I was an outsider next to anyone we were with. I was always on the edge of the conversation, in the corner of the room, never invited to join in until Lud or Aleks would appear by my side and let me feel relaxed enough to melt into them. Leander's pretentiousness, he looked down on me, and everyone could see that, so they'd follow suit. And it made me look down on myself, too.

But then there was Aleks just a few weeks after Leander and I ended. Aleks held me with pride. He still had his so-called reputation to maintain, but I was still his "cool" girlfriend who seemingly didn't care about his reputation. He included me in every conversation, introduced me to his friends without hesitation, and incorporated me into the group until I no longer questioned whether or not I belonged there, so no one else questioned it either. We loved each other quickly and easily, and that was that. There was nothing else to question, nothing to stand in our way.

Except ourselves.

I was used to being in relationships where I was the main one who didn't know how to function. I was the problem. Even while dating Jonas, he had his bad days and terrible traits, but I felt like it always came down to *me.* I was too young, or too emotional, or too damaged, or too *something* to be in a relationship. With Aleks, the playing ground was equal despite his belief that he was further enlightened than I was. He always had a bit of a superiority complex. Still, it was balanced in its own terrible way. Neither of us knew what we were doing or how to do it, not even for a second.

That's how the cycle began, starting with the Oktoberfest affair. It seemed that all my relationships were always on-again-off-again, but this was the one that hurt the most. With others, I was always heartbroken because I wanted to be wanted. Not necessarily because I wanted them. But with Aleks, I wanted *him,* wholly and entirely. And I knew he wanted me. It should've been simple with those facts alone. But it wasn't. We made it complicated.

CHAPTER 21

Meet the Parents

The day I met his family, I knew I couldn't entirely blame him. He knew about most of my history in Olímpia, the days and nights of a childhood down the drain, and he'd already met my Mom and stepdad, seeing their anxiety about me on their faces. But I only met his family months into our messy romance, after we'd made up about Oktoberfest, during a time that we weren't doing too badly. We managed to stay together without outer distractions or scaring ourselves away. Although we both knew it wouldn't last too long before we both felt chained down, we were enjoying it, and each other, while we could.

"My parents are throwing a party," he said one day as we hung out with the rest of our friends in an apartment clubhouse. The conversation had shifted away from us, and his voice was directed towards me. Still, he didn't outright invite me. I waited for him to continue, but he didn't.

"Do you…want me to come?" I finally asked.

He shrugged. "You could if you want to. Maybe you'll have fun."

Fun. It was always about fun, freedom, or whatever else made sense to him at the moment. Aleks, and our whole relationship, was made up of fleeting moments, nothing more.

112

Aleks always carried himself with an air of poshness, but not in the same way as the other rich boys. There was always something different about him, like his ego was so inflated to make up for a lack of something else. Honestly, I couldn't blame him for his cockiness–he was good-looking, played guitar and could sing well, and was the best artist I knew. He had sketchbooks on sketchbooks filled to the brim with the most amazing drawings I'd ever seen. Sometimes, when we were out in public with friends, he'd bring his guitar with him and start playing. A group would gather around to hear him sing and play, comprised mostly of girls, me included. I'd stand amongst them, watching him, catching his eye every now and then, both of us allowing ourselves a private smile. I had to keep myself from practically drooling. I couldn't believe he was *mine*, even if it was in an unconventional way. It was *our* way, and I was fine with it as long as I had him.

The party was held in a shelter at a community park. It was a casual place, but pretty. An open bar sat at one end of the room, and there was an appetizer platter in the center. Chatter and laughter echoed throughout the great space, reverberating in the empty spaces. People were dressed nicely but casually, clearly wanting to look good but not wanting to look like they tried too hard. I was glad I got the memo and followed suit, wearing my best and most casual dress.

Some of our friends were there too, so I stuck with them. This was new to me but fairly regular to them. "His parents throw a party like this at least once a year," Lud told me. "Sometimes even two. It just depends on what they feel like celebrating."

"And what are they celebrating this time?" I asked. A part of me thought they were throwing this party just because they felt like it. There were no holidays coming up that I knew of.

"His Dad launched a new newspaper," she explained. "He's giving Aleks a leading job in it."

"Oh." I definitely wasn't expecting that. Aleks wasn't really the working type. He'd recently dropped out of school and couldn't keep a job that he felt bored with, and he got bored easily if a job wasn't artistically appealing to him. He was entirely right-brained, creative to a fault, and couldn't stand doing anything that wasn't entirely in his control. But then again, I guess that would explain exactly why his Dad wanted to open a newspaper for him. Maybe it was something Aleks would finally stick to.

Aleks swung by our group, looking charming as ever in a suit. No tie, of course. That would be too strict for him. "Hey, you came," he said as he leaned in to kiss my cheek.

"Of course I did," I said, kissing him back. As I did, I saw a couple approaching us from behind him, looking all too familiar.

My first thought was that they looked like him–the sharp jawline, deadest eyes, tan skin, prominent nose. And my second thought was how *I* might look to *them*–my blondish hair brushed to the best of my capability, my borrowed black dress that didn't entirely fit me around the waist. I wasn't sure if they knew me as their son's girlfriend or their son's casual fling.

His Dad looked me up and down, and I got a similar feeling to how I felt when Aleks would look at me–like he was looking right through me. But this time, there was no comfort in it.

Aleks turned around, spotted them, and grinned. "Mom, Dad!" He kissed them both as well, and then they all lapsed into silence. His parents stood there awkwardly, clearly waiting to be introduced, but Aleks either didn't catch on or was avoiding it. His Mom cleared her throat, and he knew he couldn't wait any longer.

"Oh, this is Cris. Cristiane."

He'd never introduce me as his girlfriend, just let people make their assumptions. It was obvious we were together, anyway. They both reached to hug me politely, both leaving an air kiss on my cheek, as was the custom. Their hands were cold, opposite to Aleks's warmth. I was keeping a tally in my head of all their similarities. Looks? Check. Eyes? Check. Warmth? Nope. They were as cold as ever. I forced a smile, nervous as hell. I didn't know what kind of parents they were. Were they like my Dad and Madonna? Or my Mom and my stepdad? Or something else entirely?

"Thank you for coming tonight," his Dad said, his tone clipped. I recognized that tone. He didn't quite care if I was there or not and probably would've preferred it if I weren't. It was what he felt he had to do, what most families would feel they had to do when they first spoke to their son's maybe-girlfriend, maybe-just a thing.

I looked at Aleks nervously, who kept his eyes on his parents. I noticed that his posture was straighter, imitating his mother's. I nodded, looking back at his Dad. "Yes, of course," I said, trying to keep my voice light. "I'm happy to."

We made small talk. It wasn't the worst thing in the world. Girlfriends have definitely had worse first introductions with their boyfriends' families than that. But I had to stop myself from flinching with every word they spoke to me, all of their inane questions: "Where are you from? Where's your family from? Are you in Aleks's grade?" I knew exactly what they were doing, that same tone his Dad had. They were vetting me, trying to figure out if I was good enough to eat the food at their table, to breathe the same air as them, to kiss their son.

Aleks couldn't care less, sometimes participating in the conversation and other times talking to the rest of our friends.

That whole evening, something felt off about it. There was unspoken pressure between Aleks's family as if there was more at stake than some lavish party for a newspaper opening. I started to put the pieces together in my head: Aleks's tiny bedroom, the two-bedroom apartment they all live in, squished together. I couldn't remember what his Mom did for work, but I knew that his Dad was some sort of politician. Sure, that came with plenty of connections. But it didn't come with money.

Aleks drove me home afterward, and both of us were champagne-tipsy. He couldn't stop talking, and I loved listening.

"I know this newspaper thing is a great idea and all, but geez, this isn't the first time they've tried it," he said. "I know they want me to get into, like, a real job. Something sustainable, I guess. But that's not me, and they *know* it's not me, and I know it's not me. I just feel like I'm better than that, you know? Like, I was given all of these…gifts. My art, and all of that. I feel like I need to use *that for* something on my own. Not for…some newspaper that's not even really mine, despite what they say."

He parked the car in front of my apartment building and walked out. I did the same. I watched him as he walked up to my building, his long hair bouncing on top of his head with every step he took. I had to take bigger strides to keep up with his long legs.

"What book are you reading right now?" I asked. I'd never asked him before what he usually reads in his free time.

He seemed momentarily surprised, but only let it through for a moment before concealing it behind his usual neutral stare. "I just started it. It's about astrology, and like, how it affects us in our day to day. What it means about us, when we're born. How we're all kind of born a certain way because, well, the stars said so."

I smiled and looked up to the night sky, the moon and stars above us, and my apartment building coming up on our side of the street, looming overhead. "You'll be just fine," I said.

He gave a half-smile, appreciative. He threw his arm lazily around my shoulder and scooped me close to him to drop a kiss on the top of my head. And we were just fine.

The newspaper went broke within a year.

CHAPTER 22

Not Even the Ghosts Liked Me

With this new friend group came new experiences I never expected. Like for example, stepping back into the spiritualist life that my mother first introduced me to. It wasn't necessarily in the same way that I was used to, not nearly the same level of devotion. On the contrary, it was almost casual. Just, "Hey, do you wanna play the cup game tonight?" and we'd all get together to play as if it were a regular board game.

To summarize, the cup game was a makeshift Ouija board. Since boards did not exist in my country back then, we'd write out the letters ourselves and place a cup in the middle instead of a planchette.

Back then, everyone believed that the supposed spirits coming through a Ouija board were "good spirits." They were thought to cause no evil and do no harm, just harmless ghosts who wanted to play a game with mindless teenagers. I don't believe that anymore, but at the time, it was common sense. It felt stupid to be afraid of a cup of scary stories.

The game always started with someone asking the cup—or in other words, the spirits—if there was someone there that they didn't want in the room for whatever reason. Typically, the cup would spin on its own, directing to whoever that person may be if anyone. Most of the time, the cup wouldn't move at all in response to this question. Since these were considered to be good spirits, whoever they rejected might be considered to have bad energy. So, with my deep-rooted insecurity, you can imagine how devastating it was when the cup pointed to me the first night I tried to play.

"Aw, tough luck," one of my friends said casually from his seat on the floor next to me. He shrugged, but I felt sick.

Everyone was looking at me, and I felt my face flush red with embarrassment. Still, I tried to mimic my friend's nonchalance and attempted a shrug. "Weird coincidence," I muttered with a forced smile and made my way out of the room.

I tried to convince myself that's all it was. Just a really weird coincidence. But sure enough, the next time we tried to play, the cup once again pointed to me. And on my third try, too.

It eventually became a joke within the group that the spirits just didn't like me. I couldn't bring myself to laugh it off. It felt like more to me and lowered my already-rock-bottom confidence. I always thought there was something wrong with me, and this just further confirmed my fear. I never gave much thought to spirits, but now I wondered if they might know something that I don't. Could they see right through me, to my rotten core? Could everyone?

CHAPTER 23

The Stars Spoke

I remember cutting collards for the first time when I was 12 while living with Madonna. We had our regularly packed house of family, Madonna's friends, and a cleaner or two. Her friends were hanging around in the kitchen as she and I cooked.

I was helping with the salad, as I usually cut lettuce for each salad. This was the first time Madonna tasked me with the duty of cutting up collards. I tried to make myself as small as possible, quietly pulling out a cutting board and knife, choosing the corner of the kitchen counter furthest away from them all, my back to them. Madonna always judged everything I did, and I especially hated it when she did so publicly.

I usually cut lettuce thickly, like I was taught to. Row after row, letting the piece fall onto the cutting board. I assumed that collards had to be something like that, too. I bunched the leaves together in my left hand, pressing them against the board, and used my right hand to hold the knife and begin slicing.

I did this for only about five minutes when I heard Madonna's hideous cackle come from behind me like a truly evil stepmother would. "Oh my *goodness*, Cris, do you not know how to cut *collards?*"

I immediately felt heat rush to my face from embarrassment. It should've been a small thing–a 12-year-old not knowing how to cut collards, big deal. But Madonna had a special gift for making the mundane into the most mortifying experience.

"Are you stupid?" she proclaimed as her friends laughed along. "Who doesn't know how to cut *collards?* You must be really slow, Cris. You cut them *thinly*, hair-thin, not like that. What, you think it's like lettuce? That's so embarrassing for you."

And I did feel stupid. Really, really stupid. This is how I felt when Aleks and I broke up again for the fifth time.

I knew that we both had our own demons, mostly stemming from our families. But I quickly realized that Aleks's demons were due to the complete opposite of my situation. I was troubled due to the degradation from my family; he was troubled due to too much praise from his.

Everyone around Aleks believed that he was destined for greatness. And how could he not be? He was beautiful and talented; what else could a person need? But he didn't have the drive needed to pursue those things. Not that he needed to–his parents and friends all thought, Aleks included, that he was God's gift to Earth. He assumed, and so did his family, that his greatness would just magically allow for things to fall into place for him. But more often than not, things don't work that way.

Despite dropping out of high school and not coming from wealth, Aleks still managed to float by in life. At some point in our relationship, I began to see that he was letting the current take him wherever it wanted to while I was battling to swim upstream, against it. The odds were against me, while they favored him. They built a wall around me while they made a clear path for him.

His love for astrology ran deep, another byproduct of his hippie phase. He was convinced it would explain why

122 | Broken by Love: The Story of an Atheist Turned Pastor

we always tore our relationship apart, and ourselves along with it.

He finished reading that stupid book he'd mentioned to me before and even ordered an astrological map of his life. Then when we met the next time, we sat in that same spot we were in when everything first began. At the picnic bench, I sat on the table while he sat on the seat below me. His shoulder to my calves. He held the map in his hands. We'd been dating on and off for nearly a year at that point.

"Cris, I don't…I don't think this is ever going to work," he said. He sniffled, and I couldn't tell if he was getting emotional for once or if it was just from the cold. There was a bite to the wind tonight, and I huddled myself in my sweater. I felt nauseous and sick, knowing exactly where this was going. While dating Aleks, I felt that I knew a lot of things about him. There was always a sense of certainty. But this was both a blessing and a curse, especially in moments like this one.

"Just because some map told you that?" I muttered, bitter, trying to play as cool as he always did.

"No, I'm *serious*." He turned to look at me, and I could see his eyes were wetter than usual. "Oh. We've—we keep trying to do the same thing, over and over again, and it still doesn't work. It *never* works, and it's—it's never going to."

I felt my eyes beginning to fill as well. I tried to blink them away. "Aleks, what are you doing?"

He sighed, looking back at the map in his hands. "I've been…reading a lot, studying, trying to figure out how we can make this work. And I talked to an astrologist, and I asked her to do a map."

"A *map?*"

He nodded. "A map that tests our compatibility. Kind of a map. Between our star signs."

I closed my eyes, feeling a bit exasperated. "Aleks…"

"No, Cris, look." He opened the map and showed me the pages with his writing scrawled all over them, notes upon notes. I spotted my name a few times in the margins. And then he pulled out a piece of paper and opened it up. It was a chart of the stars, specifically the stars on the nights we were both born. "I'm trying to make you understand. Haven't you wondered why we hurt each other all the time? And still, go back to each other regardless?"

"It's just...the way we are," I answered dumbly, remembering Madonna and those stupid collards and now Aleks and his stupid map.

He shook his head. "And *why* are we that way, Cris? *Why?*"

I opened my mouth to answer, not entirely sure of what I could even say to that, but he interrupted, pointing to the pages and exclaiming, "*This* is why!"

I closed my mouth. Tried to swallow the lump that was building in my throat.

"The map...the map said," he continued, "that we're soulmates. The ultimate loves of each other's lives. And yeah, it's corny, but I believe it."

"So what's wrong with that?"

"What's *wrong* with that, is that the map also says that we can *never* be together."

I stared at him. He stared back. He seemed so determined, so unmovable. I always knew he was stubborn, but this time, *especially* this time, I wished he wouldn't.

"Never?" I asked.

"Never," he repeated.

And I couldn't help it: the tears spilled over and dripped down my cheeks, and I cried. And to my shock, he did, too.

I always knew Aleks cared about me despite his determination not to show it. So, seeing his face at that moment, so open and vulnerable, was an outward confirmation of what

I was already sure of. He loved me, out in the open. He was crying, and it was because of *me*.

We reached out to each other at the same time and held on tight. We cried a lot. I don't know for how long, but it was long enough that my eyes were swollen, my nose was stuffed, my head hurt, and all of my senses were numbed. There was only him for as long as I could latch on. As long as he'd let me.

We'd broken up plenty of times before. Night after night of break ups, taking time apart, but inevitably knowing we'd get back together. But something shifted this time, and I couldn't pinpoint what it meant. It wasn't a permanent goodbye; I knew that much at least. But the certainty I'd once felt about our relationship had dissipated, melted away on the pages he'd written all his notes on.

He wouldn't show up at my apartment door again, asking for me back. I wouldn't sit in his building stairwell alone and cry, waiting for him to come by. I'd continue wandering nights alone, aimless and crying, looking up at the sky and asking the stars why they'd give me him just to take him away again. Did I finally have my love story? But instead of the happy ending of a ROM-COM, it was the tragic Romeo and Juliet ending.

Despite all the drama of us being over, we couldn't get rid of each other that easily, no matter what the stars said.

His friends were still my friends. We'd constantly be in each other's vicinity and couldn't avoid each other even if we wanted to. And we definitely didn't want to.

I'd still see him at the park, at our usual gatherings. Playing his guitar, serenading all the girls as usual. Lud would sit by my side, fulfilling her role as the comforting friend.

"You guys will be back together before you know it," she said, but it didn't give me the same reassurance as it usually did. Maybe we would be back together soon, but it wouldn't be the same. I didn't know how to explain to her, how to put it into words, that I had a gut feeling that things couldn't magically go back to normal like they did in the past.

It was another late night when the inevitable happened. A big group of us was gathered in my apartment building's clubhouse, my Mom managed our building as well. That felt like forever ago now. His parents were strangers to me then but were recurring characters in my life now. They were polite but kept me at an arm's length, and I did the same to them. But we both believed the same thing, ultimately: I wasn't good enough for Aleks. I wondered if they were relieved at my distance lately.

I had no idea how much more recurring they were going to get.

Aleks played guitar in the front of the room again. Some people were singing along with him. I had to hold back my laughter. He hated when people sang along; he wanted the spotlight to be on him.

I hung back with Lud, chatting with some of our other friends, trying to keep my eyes and mind off of Aleks, but the task proved to be impossible. He was always there, lurking in my heart and mind.

The night went on. It got later and later. People trickled out slowly, and with every person who walked out the door, my heart skipped another beat.

There's this feeling you get when you know something's coming, even if you're in denial about it. It's the same feeling you get when you stay up in bed, lie awake at night and are unable to sleep because you have a field trip or an exam the next day. You toss and turn with the anxiety of it but also the *excitement*. Whether you love it or hate it, it's coming regardless, and you have no choice but to be ready for it.

More and more people left. My body found itself drifting towards the front of the room, where Aleks was. I tried to not-so-subtly glance in his direction, and he'd meet my eye in return. We were like magnets; we knew we'd be together eventually. It was just a matter of time.

Lud could sense what was happening, too. "I'm getting tired," she said. "Do you want to head out with me or..." She pointedly nodded towards Aleks. "Are you hanging back?"

"I'll hang back," I said, and then quickly added, "Just a little bit. I won't go home too late."

She looked me dead in the eyes. "Are you sure?" And I knew what she was really asking me. *Are you sure you want to start this cycle again?*

I gave her a half-smile. "Yeah, I'm sure." Because that was the thing with all this: No matter how different things were, or whatever that shift was, I was always sure about him.

She left. And Aleks and I stayed.

He kissed me the moment the room was empty, and the pit in my stomach filled with nothing but him.

CHAPTER 24

The Stepmom's Predictions

No, no, no. *No.* This couldn't be happening.

I stood over my bathroom sink, trying not to throw up or have a panic attack, but I couldn't stop both things from happening at once. I opened the toilet in just enough time to spew my guts out, followed by an ugly sob escaping my throat.

I'd missed my period. I was late.

I hoped and prayed it wouldn't be true, but it was the same feeling I got that night with Aleks in the clubhouse. I *knew* it. And I could be in denial about it all I wanted, but I couldn't stop it from happening.

I wore a hoodie and sunglasses when I went to buy the pregnancy test. Goiânia was a big city, but I was so used to Olímpia's lack of privacy. I didn't want to risk anything. Even as I was handing my cash over to the cashier, even as I booked it home to use the bathroom, even as I waited for the stick to show the results, and even as it came out positive, my brain was a constant chant of *No, no, no, no, no.*

But there it was, the stupid little plus sign mocking me. It was true. I was pregnant.

My mom married my dad when she was 15, and I was born when she was 17. I wasn't married, not even close, but I also wasn't 15 like my stepmom always said. So, I couldn't tell if my situation was any better.

The wooden planks of the bench were digging into my back as I stared at the sky. It wasn't as dark as it was an hour or two ago, when I took my pregnancy test. It was about 6am then, or at least I thought it was. I didn't have anything to tell me the time besides the sun making its slow climb up, up, up.

I was 16 years old, almost 17. Aleks and I had slept together weeks ago and hadn't gotten back together that night. I'd barely even spoken to him since. And to make matters worse, he had a girlfriend now. Who was also one of his sister's best friends. Great.

Somehow, my brain felt as clear as the sky. Some clouds were here and there, sure, some fear lingering on the surface. But beneath it all, there was this honest-to-God joy that I was pregnant with the baby of the love of my life. Because that's what Aleks was to me then. He was everything. And if I was going to be pregnant with anyone's kid, I wanted it to be his.

I went to school with my head held high. I planned on telling my friends. I wasn't going to hide it from anyone.

Lud was the first one I told. We stood in the corner of a hallway in between class times.

"*Oh,*" was her initial response. "Oh, *wow*. Wait, what are you going to do? You're not...I mean, are you keeping it?"

I nodded and didn't hesitate. "Yeah. I don't think I could imagine not keeping it. I mean, it's Aleks. And it's my baby. Our baby, I guess."

Her eyes searched my face with concern. "Have you told him yet?"

"Um...no."

"When did you find out?"

"This morning. And, I mean, I haven't seen him alone in weeks. It's been hard to get him by himself since..."

She nodded. "Yeah, I know. I can't imagine it's easy seeing them together."

I sighed. No, it wasn't easy. It was my personal hell, actually. But with this situation, it felt a bit easier, funnily enough. I shouldn't have felt smug about it, but I did deep down. *You might be his girlfriend, but I'm going to be the mother of his child.*

"Look, how about this: I can't drive, but a friend of mine can give you a ride after school," she suggested. "Going to his place is probably the only chance you have of talking to him alone."

Go to his apartment. Where his family was sure to be. I could already picture their judgmental eyes when I showed up on their doorstep again. But I didn't think I had a choice anymore. Lud was right; it was my only chance.

I left after lunch in a car with a guy I knew from our shared friend group, but we were never particularly close. He was just one of the only ones who had a car and could drive. We made small talk. He didn't ask any questions about why I was going to Aleks's apartment, although he knew that we were broken up. I could appreciate that much.

I took the elevator to his apartment, my heart racing more with every step I took. And the closer I got to his front door, the angrier I felt. I was surprised by my anger; I didn't really understand what it was directed towards. Was I angry that I was pregnant or angry that we weren't together? Angry that we hadn't been more careful? I wasn't sure. But I sucked it up and knocked on the door.

Seeing his Mom and sister giving me dirty looks upon answering the door just made my anger and heartbeat spike again. But a part of me understood–they had an image to maintain, and they knew I was no good for Aleks. Every time I showed up, the same old cycle would begin. Weeks of us making a mess of each other, over and over again. And he was dating a nicer girl now, someone more suited for him. Someone from a good, well-mannered family who had the best intentions for him. But they didn't believe I could ever have any of that. I knew I wasn't welcome there.

"What are you doing here?" his sister blurted out.

His Mom cleared her throat, trying to cover for her daughter's straightforwardness. "Cris, we weren't expecting you."

"I know," I said. "I'm sorry for, um, showing up. Without warning. Can I talk to Aleks?"

His sister opened her mouth to say something, but his Mom interrupted with, "Yes. Hold on." They did not invite me in but turned away to head inside.

"Actually..." They looked back at me, his Mom wearing a surprised look, but his sister looked more annoyed than anything else. I took a deep breath. "Do you mind if he comes outside?"

Despite their clear annoyance, they called Aleks over to come outside. If he was surprised to see me, he didn't show it except for the slightest raise of his eyebrows. He hesitated in the door frame but then followed me through the fire escape door, where we could talk in private.

We sat on the steps a few flights down. I sat first, and he positioned himself next to me, his long legs stretching out two steps down while mine settled on the step below us. The moment we sat down, the anger and anxiety and mess of it all got to me; it all came out of my mouth in a rush.

"I'm pregnant, and it's yours; there's no way it's anyone else's, I haven't slept with anyone else. I didn't come here to ask for help or to ask you to–to be in the baby's life or anything; I just came to give you the news."

I immediately stood up and began to walk away, my face flushed, and I was embarrassed. I didn't even take a breath while I spoke; I didn't even look at him. I didn't want to know how he'd look at me now.

But then I felt his hand on my arm, keeping me there, steady as a rock. When I turned around, he was still sitting as I stood at the bottom of the steps, and our eyes were level with each other now. I was so scared to see his face, but now, I can't remember why. He was *glowing.*

His eyes were bright, a grin spreading across his gorgeous face.

He didn't ask me any questions. He didn't give the typical, "You're pregnant? Are you sure it's mine? You haven't slept with anyone else? How many tests did you take?" that most guys his age would ask. Instead, he cupped my face in his hands like he always used to and kissed my forehead before kneeling down and placing his hands on my stomach, the same way he'd cup my face. And he kissed my stomach right there in the apartment stairs. There was no one around, but even if there were, I wouldn't be able to see anyone but him. I had tunnel vision for Aleks, and I was overflowing with love for him.

I could see it: Us, together, being a family with this sudden child of ours. Maybe his Mom would grow to like me, maybe his Dad too, maybe even his sisters. Or maybe we'd create a family entirely on our own. I didn't know what the future would hold, but I felt that I'd be okay as long as it held him.

But what I was too in love to process in the moment was that Aleks never made me any promises. He never said we'd get back together, or take care of me, or even take care of the baby. He just hugged me. And that was enough at the time.

But it couldn't be enough forever.

CHAPTER 25

She Felt Completely, Utterly Defeated

There was still someone else I had to tell about my pregnancy: my mother.

I already knew it wouldn't go well. I didn't have high hopes for it at all. All I could do was mentally prepare myself for the heartache it would cause her, that I knew would show blatantly in her expression.

I'd somewhat numbed myself to my mother's reactions to my lifestyle choices by that point. We'd been in a tug-of-war over my life ever since I first moved in with her. She'd pull me to walk the straight and narrow path, to keep my head down and do good in school, and I'd pull back and insist I had it under control, that my life was my own, that I could make my own decisions. Once I found out I was pregnant, I knew this would be the final nail in the coffin. Above all else–above my bad grades and my even worse boyfriends, my late nights out and days missing from home–*this* was the blow that would really, truly crush her. And it did.

She cried like a child when I told her. Shallow, gasping breaths, her face puffy, swollen, and red with tears, snotty and hysterical. I didn't make a move to comfort her; I just stood across the room and watched. I honestly didn't feel that there was anything else I could do. We didn't have a very affectionate relationship, after all. I'd never let her hold me before, but how could I stand to hold her now?

I have a lot of empathy for her situation now, looking back. Although I couldn't handle her reaction at the time, I understand it better. She felt completely, utterly defeated. And I was the one who did it. I made her feel that way. I moved in with her when I was just becoming a teenager, and I immediately started partying too much, got held back a year, stopped studying, and now, just like she did around my age, got pregnant by a boy who didn't really love me. After growing up my whole life hearing from Madonna and my Dad what a bad influence my Mom was, her worst fear was confirmed. I'd proved them right. And by doing so, she believed that they were right about all the rumors they'd spread about her as well. Like mother, like daughter, once and for all.

I expected all of this. The breakdown, the crying, the blame on my shoulders. What I didn't expect was what came next. Through her devastation, she pulled herself together for me. Through the turmoil I'd caused her, she never left my side.

I'd like to think she had this in her all along–the ability to stand by her daughter the way I'd always needed growing up. But it was the united struggle of teen pregnancy, the one thing we had in common, that made us really come together.

While my Mom and I grew closer, I was further away than ever before from my family back in Olímpia. I had already barely visited them before I was pregnant, and now I was afraid of seeing them, though I wouldn't admit it. I chalked it up to stubbornness–I'd gone this long without seeing them, I didn't need to see them now. But I wanted to see my little sisters and brothers. And a small part of me wanted to look my Dad in the eye and tell him that I was *okay*. He'd already heard about my pregnancy, although I wasn't entirely sure how, and

134 | Broken by Love: The Story of an Atheist Turned Pastor

now I had to prove that I could do this. Despite this similarity, I was still different than my mother. I could do better. I *was* better.

My Mom went to visit my siblings on her monthly weekend trip, and this time, I asked to come with her. It was a few months into my pregnancy already, and it showed. The bump on my stomach continued to grow bigger, and I felt heavier than I ever had in my life. I wasn't used to this extra weight and was still adjusting to the mind-blowing idea of carrying a whole other *human life inside me.* What a terrifying and pressuring concept to adjust to at only sixteen years old. I often wondered if this was how my mother felt when she was carrying me.

My Dad heard that I was coming along with my Mom to visit. I'd called when we were on our way, the aunt that I'd once tried to run away with, and she let the rest of my family know. Madonna called soon after and informed me that I wouldn't be seeing my father at all. I felt my heart drop to my stomach.

I swallowed, preparing myself for the answer I knew I'd get to my question: "Why not?"

"We won't be here," she said casually, cruelly.

I nodded, blinking away the hot tears that were rising to my face. "Where is he?"

"We left town. We planned a trip for the weekend. You can't come."

He was ashamed of me. I knew he would be, but I didn't expect him to disappear entirely. But disappearing is quite literally what he did. I didn't bother trying to see him after that, knowing that he'd just find another excuse to avoid me again.

Throughout the rest of my pregnancy, he never paid a cent to take care of me or my baby. He didn't send me letters or birthday gifts, Christmas gifts, nothing. I never received an encouraging postcard or a single word from him for the entire nine months. Or even when the baby was born. My father blocked me out of his life entirely.

For the first time, my Mom reached out to give my hand a supportive squeeze. I moved my hand away.

Still, for whatever reason I had in my young mind, I was far from kind to my mother. We didn't know how to have a stable relationship, neither one of us. I still had a lot of built-up resentment for her after being practically trained to hate her for most of my life, and she didn't have the level of maturity needed to handle a daughter with a teen pregnancy.

Despite all this, I know she did her best and was ultimately there for me when no one else was. Or at least she tried to be, but she'd picked up extra work to help me throughout my pregnancy, so I was left to my own devices most of the time. Day after day, my stomach grew more and more, and I was left alone in that small apartment. I knew how to cook and take care of a house, sure, but I knew how to do that for a non-pregnant person. A pregnancy required extra care, I knew that much, but what did that entail, exactly? I had no idea.

CHAPTER 26

A Strange Invitation and a New Family

I was about three or four months pregnant when Aleks' mom invited me to move in with her and her family. She knew my Mom was constantly out working and I was mostly on my own. She wanted to make sure that I was taken care of and eating well. I felt so grateful, and the hopeless romantic in me that I'd always been deep down resurfaced once again. Aleks was still with the same girlfriend by that point, and I didn't see him often because of it. A part of me blamed her for standing between us. *Don't you see we're trying to start a family here?* I saw this as an opportunity. Maybe once I moved in, Aleks would see how foolish he'd been and would come running into my arms, ready to take care of our child. It was so romantic. TV love stories couldn't compare to the epic love story I was dying to have with Aleks that I was sure we'd now have.

But they didn't break up. At least not right away. And even worse, he'd bring her over quite regularly, nearly every day. I could only imagine what was racing through her brain the first time she walked into the house with Aleks and saw me sitting on the couch with his mother, my swollen belly peeking out. She was polite to me despite her obvious and valid feelings about me. And I was polite as well. But I resented her, even more so after Aleks first began his nightly visits to my room.

It started soon after I moved in, too soon, like he'd been waiting all along for the perfect opportunity to pounce. He'd be with his girlfriend all day, but the moment the house would fall quiet, everyone asleep in their own beds at night, I'd hear his footsteps creaking on the wood floors, tiptoeing his way over to the girls bedroom where I slept. He'd come to my bed, hold me, kiss me, and lure me back to his room, where we'd sleep together. I'd leave around dawn and go back to my room while people were still sleeping. He told me not to tell anyone, that it was a delicate situation, that he couldn't just break up with his sister's friend. I was completely blinded by my rose-colored glasses that I'd do whatever he said. I'd do anything for him. So I didn't say a word to anyone.

Needless to say, their relationship didn't last long. It was only a matter of time when the pressure of my pregnancy was too much for both of them. I'd hear their hushed voices in his room, the tension in their conversations, clearly in the middle of a fight but not wanting anyone else to hear. So they broke up, and his sisters didn't even mind that much since they'd grown to like me more. *Yes, yes, yes.* We were one step closer to finally being together. I was overjoyed.

But he didn't claim me after their breakup. He still insisted on keeping everything hush hush. Secret rendezvous in his room every night and avoidant eyes at breakfast. He'd go out with his friends, kiss as many girls as he wanted, while I laid on the couch of his family's home, my belly growing bigger as weeks went by.

Some good still came out of all this heartache. I was so much closer to Eliza and Aleks' sisters, Maria and Lori. They saw me differently now. They were funny, kind, and so incredibly helpful and caring. They were my friends now. While men continued to break my heart, the women in my life were my sole support.

Eliza took me in as if I were her own daughter. My Mom was hustling to make money for me and the baby, and she had recently developed a new notion that she wanted to move to the US, and this fixation took up her everyday life. My Dad had abandoned me entirely, and I'd never really counted Madonna as a mother figure anyway. Eliza, Maria, and Lori became my family. It was the first semblance of structure that I'd ever had in my life.

The good, unfortunately, wasn't good enough for me to stay. Aleks started bringing girls home again. I'd hear them talking in his room, see them kissing in public, a different girl every week. It crushed me. My Mom had moved in with one of her cousins in town while she was preparing to move out of the country to the United States, so I decided to go with her, at least for a little while. I needed a break from everything, from Aleks in particular.

I think that he wanted me to want him. I was his safety net to fall back on in case he never found real love again. I was carrying his baby, after all; of course, he'd assume that I'd always be there waiting for him. I wanted so badly to prove him wrong, but he was my kryptonite. And he just couldn't leave me alone. So when I moved back in with my Mom, and he showed up at my doorstep late at night, romantic and apologetic, I invited him in.

We spent two nights together, and since I was desperate for his attention and approval, I fell for it. I let myself believe it was once again a dream come true. Aleks could never give me the fairytale I wanted, the life I dreamt of. But little Cris, the inner child in me who spent all those days sitting in front of the TV, wanted to believe that he could.

"I'm gonna come with you guys," Aleks told me as he got dressed in the morning to leave. His sisters had invited me to go camping with them for their senior class trip. Although Aleks and I weren't in school anymore, they were, and so were most of our friends. It seemed like a good opportunity to reconnect with everybody.

"Really?" I said, unable to stop my voice from sounding excited. *He was coming for* me, my heart told me, and I wasn't logical enough to stop myself from believing that. I was six months pregnant. The due date was looming over us, closer and closer with each passing day. Maybe Aleks was finally ready to step up and be a good partner and father.

I shook my head, trying to calm my heart and step back to reality. "It's kind of last minute, no?" We were leaving later that same afternoon. My bags were already packed. He'd been here for the past two days, so I wasn't sure if he'd packed yet. I doubted it.

He knew what I was thinking. "Yeah, I don't need much. I'll just run home right now to grab some things."

I nodded. I was giddy. We were all going on a trip together. Aleks, Lori, Maria, all of our friends. Like one big community, basically a family. I couldn't help but build it up in my head.

"See you later," he said, giving me a quick peck before he left. I pictured him as my husband, heading off to work in the morning as he walked out the door.

CHAPTER 27

Players Will Play

The senior class had rented a bus for the trip, so I knew everybody there, and everybody knew me. News had long ago spread that I was pregnant, so it wasn't a surprise to anyone. Most of them already knew that Aleks and I were figuring things out between us as well. It was intimidating to see so many familiar faces but also comforting. There were a handful of students who had no idea who I was and were wondering why in the world a pregnant girl was joining them on their trip, but I didn't pay them any attention.

I arrived at the same time as Maria and Lori, and they helped me with my bag. We'd agreed to share a tent for the trip, so I didn't need to bring much. Aleks had already boarded. They walked in front of me, heading to their seats as I followed behind. I spotted Aleks, taller than most of the boys on the bus, and was relieved to see the empty seat next to him. Had he saved it for me? The giddiness continued to grow.

I plopped myself down in the seat next to him and smiled. He barely looked at me, gazing out the window at nothing. I placed my hand over his and moved closer to lean on his shoulder, but before I could, he moved his hand away. I felt my heart drop to my stomach.

I looked up at him and saw him glancing around the bus, specifically turning around to stare in the back right corner. I

140

followed his gaze but only saw a couple of girls that I didn't recognize. They weren't a part of our friend group, just some classmates. But I knew he was checking if anyone had seen me touch him.

He turned back to his previous position, gazing out the window. He didn't look at me once. The bus began to move, and I kept my hands to myself for the entire ride.

The rest of the day was uneventful. We arrived at the campsite, a beautiful place in the mountains of Goiânia. The air felt fresher here, away from all the smog of the city. It was beautiful, too, the sun streaming through the trees, reaching out to touch our skin. We set up camp, Maria and Lori insisting on building our tent themselves, allowing me to get off my feet after our walk to the site. I was grateful for their consideration. I felt assured that they'd be wonderful aunts once my baby was born.

Our baby. It wasn't just mine, and Aleks would step up to the plate once the baby was born; I was sure of it. He loved me; we just had to get back into the swing of things. A child is a big thing to put on the shoulders of a teenage boy. I had to cut him some slack, right?

But it was a lot on *my* shoulders, too. I was the one carrying this human inside me for nine months. And what had he done to help?

We didn't do much that night after pitching the tents. We had a bonfire, made smores, cooked dinner, talked, and enjoyed each other's company. Aleks was with his guy friends the entire evening, paying no attention to me or even his sisters. I tried to reassure myself that it was no big deal; he was always surrounded by women in his house, so it made sense that he'd want a bit of a break from us.

I slept early that night. I could hear others staying up to talk around the bonfire couples sneaking away in the dark to get some alone time. I was used to noise and was asleep before Maria and Lori crawled into their sleeping bags.

I woke up to music playing outside at 8 in the morning and the rustle of Maria getting dressed. Lori was still fast asleep, the heaviest sleeper of the three of us. I slept uncomfortably–pregnant and camping never paired well–otherwise, I wouldn't have been up yet. I nudged her awake with my foot as I began to sit up as well. I had a feeling she wouldn't want to miss the festivities outside. And breakfast, of course.

It was still cold up in the mountains in the morning, so the early-rising seniors got the bonfire going again. Breakfast was well underway, too. They probably got up at 6 to get all this started. But judging by the hushed voices I heard late last night; I had a feeling that a lot of them hadn't slept at all.

Still, the energy was high. It was a senior camping trip, after all. The music was coming from a group of guys who had brought their guitars and cajon boxes, improvising music and making up the words as they went along. I was surprised Aleks wasn't one of them until I saw some other folks beginning to dance, and he was one of them. He offered his hand to a girl who had been sitting by the bonfire, pulling her in to join the group that continued to grow. I didn't recognize her. I felt a pang of jealousy but did my best to ignore it. It was probably nothing.

Maria, Lori, and I were drawn to the smell of breakfast food as people danced. We filled our plates while watching them with amusement, giggling amongst ourselves. Lori and I were talking to one of the girls who had cooked breakfast, complimenting her on her ability to cook the best-scrambled eggs we'd ever had. I began to glance over my shoulder back to the dancing again when Maria grabbed my arm, turned me back around, and said in a low voice, "Don't look back."

I froze. Lori looked behind me, her eyes widened with shock, and then her anger mixed with disappointment. *Oh, no.* I already had a feeling I knew what it was, but I asked anyway. "What's wrong?"

"Let's just...go eat in the tent," Lori said, linking her arm through mine. "Or take a walk."

But the suspense was killing me. I whisked around before they could stop me, and my breath caught in my throat.

Aleks, kissing the girl that he'd pulled in to dance with. A complete stranger.

The music was still playing, but it felt like it had slowed. Maybe it actually had. I looked around and saw people glancing at me, trying their best not to make it obvious, looking away when they caught my eye. There were others outright staring at me with sympathetic gazes.

Everyone here knew that I was pregnant and carrying his baby. And he was kissing a *stranger.*

I felt something shift inside of me at that moment. This was it. This was my last straw.

CHAPTER 28

I Have a Baby

My Mom put her plans of moving away on hold, for the sake of myself and the baby. She rented a two-bedroom apartment with room for us both. We shopped and decorated together, built a crib and purchased everything we needed to make it feel a little more like home, like a place I could bring a child into.

I didn't reach out to Aleks anymore. I still spent time with the women in his family–I'd grown attached to them and couldn't help but think of them as *my* family now too, even if Aleks wouldn't claim me or his child–but wouldn't talk to him in passing. I told myself that if he loved me, if he wanted a life with me and the baby, he'd begin to make an effort. But the due date arrived, and he still never did.

I decided on a C-section because it was more common in Brazil, that is what the doctors recommended back then and because I was afraid of the pain. I went to the hospital with my mother by my side and let Maria, Lori, and Eliza know that it was time. My mother stayed with me the whole time, and the girls came the next day. It was 8pm on a Thursday, and Aleks never showed. I named him Bruno, after a kid named Bruno in my building that was kind to me and gave me chocolate while I was pregnant.

Time went by in a blur. Sleeping, meeting my son, healing from the surgery, and trying to process the fact that I was seventeen years old, and I was a *mother*. I had a son, and he was mine, and he came out of me, and he was beautiful. He had my blood in him. I'd always heard that when a mother gives birth, it's the worst pain of her life until she finally holds her baby in her arms. Then, the pain magically dissipates because all you see is the child in front of you. I never believed it until I held Bruno. The rumors were true: he was everything.

It was crazy to think about. But underneath the joy of having Bruno, there was the haunting fact that he had parts of his father in him, too, a boy who didn't even want to see him.

Two days had passed when Aleks finally showed up. It felt like a doctor's visit–cold, detached, quick. I wondered where the warmth of first love went when it had disappeared completely. And I hated my own surprise at the fact that he'd bothered to show up at all. It was rodeo week again, and I knew he'd be going to that. I thought back to the rodeo I went to when I was 13. It seemed so long ago now. I wondered if that was when my bad taste started or if it had always been bad. I used to love sweet boys like Massimo. Now, I love boys like Aleks, who got girls pregnant and didn't bother to show up to their son's birth. When had that changed? And why?

Aleks was there for five minutes. He didn't ask to hold Bruno, I had to offer. He didn't ask his son's name; I had to tell him. And then he was out the door, going to drink and hook up for the weekend. In that moment, I almost hated him.

After a few days in the hospital, I went home to heal and take care of Bruno; I hadn't registered his birth yet because I wanted to give Aleks the opportunity to reach out and do it with me. In Brazil, the father has to *want* to claim their child. And if not, their name won't even be placed on the birth certificate. I decided that this was it. It was completely in his hands.

I waited fifteen days. Fifteen depressing days of just wanting the father of my child to *want* their child. And, honestly, a selfish part of me wanted to see if he'd want me, too. But the more time that passed, the angrier I became. I snapped out of my lovesick trance for Aleks. How *dare* he put me in this position and take zero accountability for it?

I went to the notary and registered the birth certificate with only *my* name on it.

I let his family know because I thought it would be better if they heard it from me. I knew it would hurt them. I knew they'd feel betrayed. They'd done *so* much for me throughout my pregnancy, and I owed a lot to them. But at the end of the day, it wasn't about them anymore. It was about Aleks and his decision to not want his own son. Eliza, Maria, and Lori tried to talk me out of it. Because, in a way, it was like saying that they didn't have any claim to Bruno either, although that wasn't how I felt. I'd always consider them to be his aunts and Eliza to be his grandmother, even if it wasn't on paper.

"Look, if he wants to go and claim his son any time, he can," I finally told them. "I won't stop him. But I'm also not going to do it for him. It's up to him."

That seemed fair for everyone. But days turned into weeks, turned into months. Bruno's birth certificate continued to only have my name on it. Although I said I'd given up on Aleks, a part of my heart was holding out that one day, he or his sisters would call and say he'd gone to the notary to do his part. But he never did.

CHAPTER 29

Reality Started to Set In

My Mom moved to the United States when Bruno was about six months old. She rented a bedroom for Bruno and me in an apartment near Eliza's apartment, and the other room was rented to another student. I continued to live close to Maria, Lori, and Eliza because they were now my main and only support in the area–they'd babysit Bruno while I was job-hunting, grocery shop for me when I had my hands full with him, and we'd regularly have dinner together in my apartment. I was thankful for their support despite Aleks's incompetence. Although we'd been brought together under tough circumstances, they were family now.

I'd long since dropped out of school to focus on surviving and raising Bruno. But I still saw Aleks everywhere. At grocery stores, on walks, whenever I'd visit his sisters, and always with a new girl under his arm. I wondered if he'd gotten any of them pregnant. He'd never come to see Bruno at my place, would only spend time with him when I brought him to Eliza's home, and even then, he'd leave quickly. And despite my anger and growing resentment towards him, it gutted me.

I'd been hurt since I was born without ever getting a break in life. I was in a constant tug-of-war with the people I loved most in life, who I couldn't figure out how to love correctly,

147

who I felt didn't love me back as much as I did them. And all I'd ended up with was calloused hands and a tired heart. My relationship with most of my family was ruined–Mom, Dad, Madonna, my brothers, and I barely saw my little sisters–and despite my fascination with ROM-COMs and determination to have my own one day, I'd still always come up short. Was I the only thing in common with all the bad things that had happened to me? Was it my fault?

Bruno was the only good thing to come out of all this. In my loneliness, he brought me comfort. He was the light of my life, and I thrived to be his. So, no matter how depressed I was, I'd smile for him. I tried to not let myself traumatize him the way my stepmom did me. But when I put Bruno down to sleep, I'd cry. All the hurt that had been building up over my entire life was finally getting to me. I'd pushed it down, projected it onto others, had given myself no room for grief. Now, all I had was room. And I realized that I couldn't run from it anymore.

My aunt reached out to me around the same time I came to this realization, my mother's sister, a different one than the one I'd tried to run away with years ago. She wanted to meet Bruno and help alleviate things for me. "I'll rent an apartment for you, near me, and I can watch Bruno while you job hunt," she told me. She'd since moved further away from Olímpia, about an hour out of the city. I'd be just out of reach of Madonna and Dad. On the other hand, I'd also be away from Maria, Lori, and Eliza. *But* I thought to myself, *I'll be far from Aleks, too.*

Despite how much I loved being with my friends and Bruno's aunts, Goiânia felt different now. Basically, I'd lived the entirety of my teen years there, and now that I was a mother, I felt more grown up. Almost adult-like. I couldn't relate to people my age anymore. I'd see them in the town squares, hanging out in the building's lobby. The student who roomed with me would bring a friend or two over sometimes, and I'd hear their laughter floating through the apartment like a ghost of my past. Everyone seemed so young, even if they were older than me. And even though Maria, Lori, and Eliza felt like family to me now, the hard truth was that they were my *ex's* family. An ex I couldn't stand to even look at. I didn't want to depend on them anymore.

I started packing my things as soon as I hung up the phone.

I didn't have enough money to sustain myself and a child, and I knew I desperately needed a job. My Mom sent me money every month from her new job in the US, but it wasn't nearly enough. I was grateful to have a roof over my head, thanks to my aunt, but I didn't want to just survive. I wanted my child to have the life he deserved.

I was responsible by then—I didn't drink or smoke and had long ago given up on dating (although my tendency of being a romantic refused to go away; I was still an avid ROM-COM watcher). Still, no one wanted to hire an eighteen-year-old single mother who had dropped out of high school. I'd given up on the lack of job opportunities in Goiânia and hoped São José do Rio Preto might open new doors.

I felt like a mother before I even turned ten years old. By the time I was 10, Madonna had her first child, a baby girl, and it was my responsibility to check on her in the middle of the night when she cried and soothe her back to sleep. It was my responsibility to make sure that she was taken care of, fed, and raised correctly. I helped raise her in the early years of her childhood until I left to move in with my mother. My guilt in leaving her and my other sister was immense, only adding to my fear of motherhood. But it had given me the experience of learning to take care of a child and myself at the same time, and I called upon those memories as I raised Bruno. I'd felt like a mother before, but now I *was* one. The sacrifice of my childhood was one thing; I was making a whole lot of other sacrifices now.

Looking for work as a young single mother proved to be one of the biggest challenges I faced. I went back to school in the meantime. Job hunting by day, classes at night. It took so long that it was to the point where my family thought I wasn't looking at all anymore or just killing time. I couldn't blame them for thinking that, considering the way I'd acted the past few years. But I wished they could see how much effort I was really putting in, how I was actively working towards building a future instead of just passing the time. I wanted a life, and this time, I didn't want it just for myself.

After months of feeling like my efforts were coming up to nothing, my Mom came to visit. She'd found a job in the US and found a place for herself. I saw an opportunity, and I reached for it immediately. I asked her to let me leave the country and move in with her. She agreed and got to working on getting me a visa.

CHAPTER 30

Moving to the U.S.

America's slogan is all about freedom, but I spent my first two months locked up watching TV. It was boring, to a point, near misery, but I didn't mind as much as I thought I would. I got to bond with Bruno and catch up on all my beloved ROM-COMs that I hadn't had time to watch. It fed the romantic in me that I thought had died with Aleks. I let myself sink into the comfort of them, making sure to keep closed captions on to help me learn English faster. Thanks to my resurfaced addiction, I could understand English enough to get a job after two months.

I still didn't have my driver's license or any fluency in English, but my Mom got me a job at a perfume distributor where she worked. I made a measly $200 a week and had to pay a babysitter another $100 to watch Bruno during the day. A friend I made in the neighborhood had a job cleaning banks at night and paid me $50 a week to help her. On weekends, I'd bus tables at an Italian restaurant in Boca Raton. But no matter how much I worked, I didn't have enough to survive, and I felt like I wasn't getting anywhere.

I met Daniel in my neighborhood in my first week there. If I'm being completely honest, I met his friend first, who was visiting from out of town, and was immediately interested. But his friend left after a week, and from what Daniel had told me, he'd asked his friend for permission before pursuing me: "Hey, if you're not interested in her, I am." And he quickly began hitting on me after his friend gave the go-ahead. But unlike my feelings towards his friend, I just wasn't interested in Daniel, no matter how hard he tried. And he tried *really* hard.

Dating Daniel was like waving a white flag. If persistence were a person, it would be him. He was never harsh or rude about it, but he was consistent in his romantic gestures, and he treated Bruno with so much kindness that I felt like a villain if I shot him down. So I stopped shooting him down and decided to just go with it. Maybe a relationship with him wouldn't be so bad. But, as you already know, I was always a romantic, and it was difficult to date someone I didn't really feel anything towards.

After about a month of working and dating Daniel on and off, I still wasn't anywhere near where I wanted to be financially, but I felt that maybe I was okay and could build a life here. But this feeling didn't last long because as soon as my mother thought that I made enough money, she asked me to contribute to pay rent.

I was furious. I didn't think she was wrong for asking me to pay rent, necessarily, but I was angry at her poor timing and, in my eyes, heartlessness towards my situation. I was eighteen, in a new country, trying to raise money for myself and my son. I'd only been there three months and was in no position to pay rent. And she would never help me with Bruno, even at night when she was home. I had to pay a stranger to stay with him so I could work. But if I had to pay rent anyway, I told her I'd rather live with a stranger. And I did exactly that for about two weeks until I realized how uncomfortable it was to rely on strangers for everything. Even though I'd paid them for the room, I felt like an intruder everywhere I went.

One day, Daniel came over to spend time with me and Bruno. He sat on the floor with my son, playing with him while I sat on my bed and tried to relax for once. I watched them, how easily they got along, the smile Daniel brought to Bruno's face. I was so busy trying to provide for Bruno that I rarely had the energy to really play with him. I envied that. But more than envy, I realized how much it was a necessity to have this in my day-to-day. I wanted him to become a routine. Not for myself, for Bruno.

"What if we moved in together?" I blurted out.

Daniel looked up at me from his spot on the floor, his eyebrows raised in surprise, but not as surprised as I thought he would be. "Yeah?"

I nodded. "Yeah.

He smiled. He hesitated; he thought it was too soon. But he would do anything for me.

I moved in with Daniel for stability and consistency, and we definitely had that. We fought very consistently. It was more like bickering, and with every argument we had, I grew increasingly irritated with him. He didn't necessarily do anything bad, but living with someone I couldn't have feelings for wore my patience thin. Everything he did was frustrating, even when he meant well. So we'd fight because he'd get annoyed at my annoyance, and we'd fall into this endless cycle: I'd leave him, he'd make some grand romantic gesture to win me back, and I'd convince myself that maybe this time I could really develop feelings for him. And we'd try again. Wash, rinse, repeat.

One time, during a brief break-up period, I'd gone to his car to gather my things, particularly Bruno's car seat. And there, sitting in the car seat, was a teddy bear holding a bouquet of flowers and a handwritten love letter. When I came back, he was making sandwiches for my next shift at work, tucking a note into the brown paper bag like he always did. And I was reeled back in, just like that.

Still, my love for him never grew. I loved him but was never in love with him. I kept waiting for it to happen, for something to just *click* and make me fall in love with him, but it never did. And I tried, for a year. We tried to build a life together, for our sake, for Bruno's. But it never clicked.

After nearly two years, I was burnt out, exhausted, and still broke. It wasn't worth so much effort when I ultimately found myself back in the same place I was while living in Brazil. I'd moved to the US hoping I could find a job along with the help of my mother, but I was convinced that she didn't have a maternal bone in her body. She'd get upset at me for turning away from her but then would do the same to me when I reached out. I opened the door for a relationship, and all she did was make excuses. When Daniel and I both worked nights, I had to rely on strangers to watch Bruno. At least in Brazil, I had more family to support me. Or, at the very least, I'd have Maria, Lori, and Eliza. And that was more than enough for me.

Leaving your country feels like the worst possible thing. When you first depart, you can't imagine any other place in the world except what you've always known. But the worst thing is when you go back.

CHAPTER 31

Back to Brazil

I didn't realize how difficult it would be to readjust, and in the end, I only lasted two months. Two eventful months, to say the least.

I moved back in with my aunt while I gave job-hunting another chance, of course to no avail. Out of a need for my son to know his family, I reached out to my Dad. Bruno was two years old by then. I swallowed my pride and went to visit them in Olímpia.

Seeing the streets I used to run through, felt like another life. Running around downtown with neighborhood kids who barely liked me, wanting so badly to be liked by them. My childhood crush on Massimo, and what it was like to visit him again after so many years and be so deeply disappointed. I wondered what it would have been like to have had a *real* life here, a real childhood, instead of the forsaken one I'd ended up with.

Despite everything Madonna had put me through, I was excited to let her see my son and have her hold him. A part of me still itched for her approval, like I always used to. If her approval was a drug, I was an addict who hadn't had a fix in years. I was ready to relapse.

Madonna scooped Bruno up in her thin arms, cradling him close to her chest. It seemed natural to her, but every nerve in my body tensed up at the sight of it. I was on edge the whole time she held him, bouncing my leg up and down to shake some of the nerves out of my system.

"You know," Madonna began, "lots of people go to the US and leave behind their kids with the rest of their family. So they can, you know, settle in on their own, and then bring their kids when they're ready. Why don't you try it?"

I was nineteen with a two-year-old son, and my stepmother was making a suggestion I never would've dreamt of in a million years. If anyone else had said that to me, I wouldn't consider it even for a second. I'd feel that I was abandoning my son the way my Mom had abandoned me. But because it was *Madonna* who had said it, the woman who had manipulated me to my core and whose acceptance I craved more than anyone else's, it seemed like the perfect idea.

I left for São Paulo the next day while Madonna watched Bruno, staying there for around three days to secure another visa since my last one had expired. By the time I got back, my application process was complete, and Madonna had changed her mind about taking care of Bruno. "I've already sacrificed my life for kids before; I'm not going to do it again." Looking back, I realize that was the best thing that could have happened to me. How could I even consider leaving my child with Madonna.

I was put straight back into a cycle of loss and confusion. I wasn't sure what to do with my life anymore, and the future was more uncertain than ever. Most other people my age had the same feelings, but it was about college and careers. Mine was about survival. I went back to Rio Preto with my fingers crossed, hoping that a big city would provide more opportunities.

As soon as I got back before I even began job-hunting again, I told my grandma about what Madonna had suggested, expressing my frustrations about her last-minute reversal. "You could still do it," my grandma said, and I looked at her in shock. She shrugged casually, as if big life changes like this happen all the time. "You could leave him with me and your aunt. You know I already take good care of him. It won't change much."

Except, of course, it would change everything. And a part of me knew that. But this was the only light in the tunnel within my reach.

I moved back to the US again, this time without Bruno. It left an ache in my heart and a pit in my stomach, but I told myself over and over that this was for the best. It had to be. There had to be a reason for all of this.

CHAPTER 32

Back to the U.S.

Before getting back to the US and making the final decision to leave my son behind, Daniel reached out to me and asked for another chance. I told him of my grandma's proposal and told him very clearly that if I go back, it is to make money so I can bring my son as soon as possible. Daniel wanted to get back together immediately, but I gave him a condition: we'd get back together if we moved to New York, where he'd previously lived. Florida was overpopulated with immigrants like me trying to make a living and build their futures, but Daniel had previously told me he'd made more money in New York. This was my shot. I was coming back, but I refused to stay stagnant again. I was there with a plan and a mission to have my son by my side as soon as possible.

Unfortunately, having a plan doesn't mean much when it's continuously thwarted by those you rely on. I moved into Daniel's small apartment in Florida, expecting us to move to New York any day now. It was my only condition for our relationship, and I trusted that he would respect it. But days turned into weeks turned into months, and nothing changed. I kept bugging him, asking when we were going to make plans to actually move, but he always said that he was working on it. He pushed plans back more and more, and our move to New York was nowhere in sight.

I knew Daniel well by this point, had learned his ins and outs, and I had a growing feeling that we weren't going anywhere. He was born in the US and grew up in Brazil before coming back to New York in his 20s. His grandmother had practically raised him while he was in Brazil, and she had passed away a few years back. When her condition was worsening, his family asked him to come back to Brazil to see her. And he put it off, again and again, until she was gone. He never saw her again. And I knew that was exactly the type of person Daniel was—someone who was terrified of change, who would never take risks, who would root himself to the ground if he could.

I couldn't blame him entirely for our conditions. I could've picked up and left if I wanted to, but I didn't know how. We were hours away from New York, and I didn't have money, couldn't drive anywhere, and had no idea how to even begin apartment hunting. I felt trapped, and it was my own doing. After three months of Daniel and I going in circles, I broke up with him and moved back to Brazil again. Because if I was going to be poor, at least I would be poor with my son by my side.

CHAPTER 33

She is Just a Friend

It didn't take long for him to start calling me, day after day, over and over, begging for me to come back and get back together.

"Will we go to New York?" I demanded, fed up. "And I mean it. I can't stay in Florida anymore."

"Yes, yes, of course, I'm already looking for jobs," he said. "I mean it. I'd do anything for you."

I knew he meant it. Daniel hadn't proven himself to be very reliable, but he'd consistently shown his love for me. It was the only thing I could count on, and I clung to it. We started dating again, long distance, and began making plans for me to come back to the US.

Around this same time, Eliza reached out to me after hearing I was back. "It's been so long since we've seen Bruno and you!" she said over the phone. "Come visit; you can stay with us for a few days. We miss you two."

I had time to kill before moving back with Daniel, and I missed them as well. Despite not having seen them in a while, they were still some of my dearest friends. And after all, Bruno was theirs, too, despite Aleks's refusal to claim him.

But once I arrived, I found that maybe that wasn't entirely true. At least, not anymore. While Eliza was fussing over

160

Bruno, catching up on some much-needed Grandma time, Lori pulled me aside.

"I wasn't sure if I should tell you this or not," she began, "but since Aleks is out of town for now, I figured you needed a heads up before he got back. So you have time to think about it."

I was as confused as ever, unsure as to what this news might possibly be. "Think about what?"

"First, I want you to know that he's not out of town on purpose; he didn't know you were coming," she rambled. She bit her lip, but her eyes were lit up, simultaneously nervous and giddy at once. "He said he wants to change his life for real this time. He wants to…take things more seriously, and he wants to take things more seriously with you." My heart skipped a beat, but I waited for her to finish. "He said he figured out that you're the love of his life and that—that he'd do *anything* for you guys to be together."

I couldn't help it—a grin stretched across my face, the biggest I'd smiled in months, maybe years. Daniel had never made me smile that much, no matter how much he'd tried. And he'd tried a lot. I started dreaming of what my and Aleks's life could be like together, imagining moving to the US together with Bruno, or maybe just staying here with his mother and sisters, and finally being united as a family together. My son could finally have a father.

But I was still hesitant, with one foot out the door. I'd been hurt too many times in my life, most of all by Aleks. My heart was in defense mode, and I had my guard up. I'd gone nearly two years without Aleks—I could go with more if I had to, although I really, *really* didn't want to anymore.

Aleks returned two days later. He looked somewhat different, his hair longer and his arms bigger, looking more like a hippie than ever. He dropped his travel bag on his bedroom floor, turned to me, and immediately told me almost exactly what Lori had already said, but with some extra words, I needed to hear. "I love you," he proclaimed with the same confidence I remembered. "I-I always have, and I've tried to love other people as much as I love you, but…I can't. No one compares. You're the—the love of my *life*. And I want to be with you and Bruno. I want to marry you, and move to the US with you, and start our lives together. For real this time."

And there it was, happening all over again. I melted into him like I always did. I called Daniel and broke up with him over the phone that same day.

I was at the point where I'd do absolutely anything to fix my life, and I wanted to do it along with Aleks, to give Bruno his real father instead of a placeholder. So, even with my hesitation and doubts, I moved back in with Aleks's family, and Aleks and I began the process of trying to get our visas again together.

I tried to achieve a life of semi-normalcy, as normal as a 19-year-old single mother could. I tried to find a balance between being a mom and having a personal life, with the help of Eliza whenever she was willing to watch Bruno. I tried to come up with odd jobs to scrape in some cash whenever I could, and I tried to have fun in the meantime.

I couldn't deny that it was wonderful being back in Goiânia with Aleks again. Going out into the town with friends, feeling eyes on us that weren't eyes of judgment for once, but admiration. We had a son together. We were practically a family, and everyone knew it. The love I had for him was written all over my face.

Aleks and his sisters had become good friends with a group of girls in town, most of which were housemates together and attending the local city college. They were eager to introduce me to their new friends, gushing about how much I'd love them, that I'd fit right in. So, one night when Eliza was kind enough to watch Bruno again, we went out on the town.

We met the girls at their apartment for a night in. I felt like I had a part of my life back in a way, but at the same time, it was a life I wasn't really a part of anymore. It was comforting to be in an environment so familiar despite never having been to this particular home before. But the bustle of people around, the smell of beer—half of me felt reassured by how normal it felt, and another half of me felt like a puzzle piece that had been put in the wrong box. I was a mother, I'd lived outside of the country, and my worldview had expanded immensely compared to college kids who had barely ever left town despite us all being around the same age. I didn't know how to fit in here anymore.

However, the girls I was introduced to were nice and did their best to make me feel comfortable despite my self-consciousness. One of the housemates arrived later in the evening, her hair windblown and her eyes searching the room until they landed on Aleks. Her face lit up immediately, and my heart dropped.

She came up to our group, standing in a circle talking. She threw her arms around Aleks first, who immediately reciprocated the hug for a bit too long. I stood next to him awkwardly, but as I looked around, no one else seemed to think this was out of the ordinary, which only made me more uncomfortable.

Once they finally released each other, she greeted Maria and Lori before turning to me. Lori linked her arm through mine, which made me drop a bit of the tension from my shoulders. I knew that they'd tell me if there was something I really needed to worry about.

"Karen, this is Cris!" Maria introduced me excitedly. Her giddiness almost matched Lori's when she first told me the news about Aleks.

Karen's eyes widened, and she briefly looked me up and down in a way that I don't think anyone else would've noticed if they weren't already suspicious of her. And I definitely was. Her mouth broke out into a smile, and she reached to hug me. "Oh, it's *so* nice to meet you! I've heard so much about you!"

I was polite, of course, and she seemed like a genuinely nice person. But the moment that I could talk to Aleks out of earshot from anyone else, I immediately asked, "She has feelings for you, doesn't she?"

He looked at me dumbfounded. "How did you know?"

I knew that he was just shocked at the fact that I'd caught on, and it made me feel small. Did he think I was stupid? "It's obvious," I said with a shrug, trying to act as nonchalant as I could. *No biggie, you just might be cheating on me again, but this time, our son is actually in your life, and we're making plans to move to the US together. It's totally fine.* "It's written all over her face. She's bad at hiding it."

He threw his arm around me and kissed the top of my head. "You have nothing to worry about; she's just a friend," he said. But I'd heard that before.

The red flags only got redder when Karen showed up at Aleks's house one day bearing a basket of breakfast goodies. Coffee, cheese bread, the works. Aleks answered the door with a smile too big for my comfort.

"Karen!" he exclaimed, pushing his bedhead out of his eyes. I felt a pang of resentment at how excited he sounded. "What's all this?"'

"Oh, you know," she said sheepishly, keeping her eyes on Aleks the whole time and not glancing once in my direction.

But I could feel her awareness of my presence as I came to stand next to Aleks, her stubbornness to not look at my face. She was shameless. I was flushed with anger and turned to grab my coat as I heard Aleks invite her inside.

I had one foot out the door when Aleks finally turned away from Karen and her stupid basket long enough to ask me where I was going. "Out," was all I said in response, because I truly didn't know where I was going. I just had to get away from the scene that was unfolding in front of me.

I took a walk through town and decided to take the opportunity to run errands I'd been meaning to do. Pick up things for Bruno, get groceries that the house was running low on. Since Eliza was kind enough to take me in while Aleks and I were figuring out our visas, and our relationship, I wanted to take on whatever responsibilities I could. Over an hour had passed when Aleks found me.

"Hey," he said, jogging to catch up to me. I didn't stop for him. He was breathless, but a part of me suspected that it was just for show; I doubted he'd been looking for me that long. "Hey, why'd you leave?"

I stopped for a moment, stunned by his statement. "Are you serious? You're joking, right?"

He shook his head, his still-messy hair moving with his motions. He furrowed his eyebrows in confusion. "No, what? Why would I be?"

"Aleks, this girl I just met, and who we both know is in *love* with you—"

"Love is a strong word—"

I glared at him. "She showed up with a *breakfast basket*. And she knew that I live with you, and she didn't even offer anything to me."

"Because you left!"

"Why would I *stay*?"

He shrugged. "You know, you could've marked your territory."

My jaw dropped. "What?!"

"Of course!" he insisted.

"Aleks, I'm not a *dog!* Mark my territory? Really?"

"No, it's not like that, listen." He paused, gently placing his hands on my arms reassuringly, looking me in the eye as we spoke. "Everyone knows that we're together, okay? But you just have to *show* that. Of course, some girls are gonna hit on me. So what? That's where *you* have to step up."

I thought it was ridiculous. Why should I have to stake my claim? I gave birth to his *son*. There shouldn't have been any more territory to mark. But there always was with Aleks. It was the same mentality he'd had when we were teenagers— the disdain for being tied down, the refusal of accountability. I should've taken it as a sign right then and there that he was the same person he'd always been, but instead, he wore me down by talking in circles, like he always did.

I think that, in my whole life, there were two people who manipulated me the most. The first was Madonna. The second was Aleks.

CHAPTER 34

The Red Flags Were All Over the Place

Aleks and I went to Brasilia, where the nearest consulate was to Goiânia. The plan that we'd settled on was that we'd get married, Aleks would finally put his name on Bruno's birth certificate, and then we'd get our visa to fo to the US.

But I quickly began to feel the same way I felt as a child, living with my Dad, Madonna, and my brother under their patriarchal rule. My brother would never help with anything around the house, leaving everything to me, from small things like basic chores to bigger things like taking care of our little sister. I used to ask him for help when I was younger, but I didn't yet know the extent of my Father's influence on him. But in our home, housework was beneath men. It was always left in the hands of a woman, while the men just pushed away any semblance of responsibility. Just like Aleks was doing.

I'd continuously asked him when we were going to get married going to city hall and just getting it over with wasn't necessarily romantic, but at least it would be done. And he'd also be able to sign the birth certificate while we were there. Two birds, one stone. But instead of just complying with something we could get done in an afternoon, he pushed it back

167

more and more, always coming up with a new excuse. Our trip to the consulate had been creeping up on us, and I was getting antsier with every day that passed. Until he showed up with a marriage certificate in hand and asked me to sign it.

"Don't I need to go to city hall to do this?" I asked. "Like, we need an officiant. A witness?"

"No, no, it's not real," he said casually, but his words hit me like bricks.

"Wait, then why am I signing this? And where did you get this?"

"Don't worry about it. This is just to make sure that we can get the visa."

"But this wasn't what we talked about, Aleks; we're supposed to go to the US as a *real* couple."

"We're still a real couple!" he said, talking me down as he always did. "It's just a piece of paper! This way, we can get married for *real* when we have money. It'll rush us less, give us more time to relax."

"I don't want to relax," I said. "I want to get my life together. For Bruno."

"We're still doing that. This is just a faster way to get there."

I didn't understand how it was any faster; it just sounded like another one of his excuses. I refused to use the fake marriage certificate because I was afraid of getting in trouble using it one day, so I settled for going as single. I knew he was too stubborn to budge, so I focused my efforts instead on trying to get him to sign the birth certificate. But as we walked into the consulate, my shoulders were heavy with the knowledge that my son, legally, still didn't have his father.

Once we got to the consulate, Aleks stepped back almost cowardly, I thought his actions were really weird. I took over to smooth it out and secure our visas. As soon as we exited the building, Aleks headed straight for a payphone, radiating success. He punched in his Dad's number, grinning from ear to ear.

"Dad, I did it!" he announced. "I got the visas!"

And maybe it shouldn't have bothered me that he didn't mention me. He took all the credit for our acquired ticket out of the country. But I couldn't help it—it did. And, like I always did, I pushed it aside.

I've read somewhere before that people who have been abused in one way or another—whether emotionally, physically, or mentally—are drawn to those who have similar personalities to their abusers. I often wonder if that's why I was drawn to Aleks.

CHAPTER 35

The Cycle Started all Over Again

We began our life in the US similarly to how I'd started it before, twice already, with some odd adjustments. Bruno stayed in Brazil with Eliza and his loving aunts while Aleks and I moved in with my mother in Florida. After everything that had happened, I didn't know what my mother currently thought of Aleks, and it was nerve-wracking to live in such close quarters, measuring her reactions to every step he took. Even more awkward was having her new boyfriend living with us, but naturally, I was sure she had the same thoughts towards me. We were both navigating these new relationships, as well as our mother-daughter relationship with one another.

The last time I heard from Daniel was through a letter. He asked me again to get back together, insisting that I was just fooling myself by being with Aleks, that I was just going to get hurt again and that Daniel was the more stable option between the two. I'd previously told Daniel about everything I'd been put through, and now I felt like he was trying to hold it over me. I didn't care enough to listen to his warnings, mainly because I never really liked him as much as he wanted me to. My heart, for better or for worse, had been with Aleks since the moment I'd met him. I didn't respond to his letter, and I never saw him again.

My Mom called some people she knew and quickly found a job for Aleks while I picked up odd jobs here and there, mainly revolving around babysitting and cleaning houses. I felt hopeful in the beginning, like this was really the start of something great. But within only eighteen days of moving to the US, Daniel's prophecy turned out to be true: Aleks broke up with me and moved out of the house to a friend's apartment, a friend he had just met recently through work. And then, a few days later, he apologized and begged to have me back.

In a way, I was right that this was the start of something. It was the start of a long and turbulent, on-again-off-again relationship with Aleks. It was the start of the longest two years of my life, and the slow realization that Aleks never really wanted to be with me again. He wanted a ticket out of Brazil, and I was it.

But throughout our tumultuous relationship, I still had a son to take care of. I still had goals and aspirations. The thought of bringing Bruno to be with me was the only thing getting me through day after day, break up after break up. I kept working towards a semblance of stability that never seemed to come. I sent some of my money to Eliza, to take care of Bruno, while Aleks never sent anything. We'd come to live in a foreign country together, but I felt more alone than ever.

I switched from babysitting to house cleaning, and as my wages went up, so did the possibility of seeing Bruno sooner. It motivated me even more. I picked up extra shifts, working day at night, taking almost any job that was offered to me. And finally, after six months, I could afford to bring my son to live with me.

Aleks and I had moved out of my mother's apartment already and gotten our own place. I had to beg him to do so, practically forcing him to chip in for rent. He was frugal, saving all of his pennies, although I didn't know for what. I went to Brazil to get Bruno, and Eliza decided to come as well. She'd done so much for me that I wanted to do whatever I could to help her have a better life as well. Besides, it seemed cruel to separate her from Bruno when she'd raised him for so long.

I wanted to bring Bruno into a life of stability, but I began to settle into the reality that this was as stable as it was going to get. Aleks and I still fought and broke up all the time, but at least we had jobs. We had a roof over our heads, and we could afford to feed the family we had. It was enough for me.

Two months later, Maria and Lori came to live with us, along with a friend of theirs I hadn't expected to see. She was introduced to me as one of their best friends, and I remembered seeing her around in the friend group we shared during the short months I lived with them while trying to get our visas.

All of the women who'd moved in were still learning the lay of the land, let alone the language, and so we were all dependent on each other for some time. After a particularly bad fight with Aleks, he apologized and said he wanted to come clean so we could have a fresh start; he confessed to sleeping with his sister's friend during the time we broke up, which was just a couple of weeks, confirming a suspicion I'd already had. Coming clean wouldn't fix anything; Aleks knew that. I think he just wanted to dig the knife in deeper.

We broke up again, naturally. I kept my distance for a few weeks, as I'd learned to do by then. I cried on my own time, away from Aleks, not out of pride, necessarily, but more out of a fear of him seeing me cry that had been ingrained in me. Every time he saw me cry, I felt little to no comfort from him. He always used it to embarrass me further, insisting that my tears were due to the guilt that it was *my* fault and not because he'd broken my heart again. But even then, I knew it wasn't the end of us. Not yet. A part of me still hadn't given up on him, and I knew I wouldn't let go of him until that part of me had died. And it was a slow and agonizing death.

The usual happened: after some time apart, he begged for my forgiveness and said he'd made a mistake. "I'm not like that anymore," he tried to convince me. "I don't *want* to be like that anymore. I only want you."

He treated his love for me like it was a new habit he was trying to get used to. Like cutting calories or waking up early. Something you don't actually want to do, nor do you plan on sticking with it. But you could do it if you have to, for a little while, at least. That's what it felt like to be "loved" by him. And still, I took him back.

Two years passed, and suddenly, I was in my 20s still begging the boy I loved when I was fifteen to love me back. Or to at least care about me, about my life and our son. I just needed *something* from him at that point, *anything,* some semblance of reassurance.

When I was first trying to get everything together in my life, I could console myself with the fact that Bruno wouldn't remember most of it. He was too young, still a baby when I first had to leave him to come to the US, and still too young to remember Daniel and our strange relationship. But now, as I was getting older, so was he. He could walk and talk, and my old consolation now grew into my biggest fear. Would he remember his lack of a father figure for so long? Or, even worse, would he remember the absent father that he currently had?

These were the concerns spinning in my head when Aleks and I went through another breakup. Everything was heightened this time. He told me that this wasn't like our usual break ups, and it shook me to my core. I didn't know what he meant, and I was terrified to find out.

CHAPTER 36

Wasn't She Just a Friend?

Usually, when we'd break up, he'd move in with Eliza and his sisters for a few days until we made up and he came back to me. So when I went to drop Bruno off in the evening before going to my second job, my heart sank when I saw the pity written all over Eliza's face as she answered the door.

She didn't ask me how I was. She scooped Bruno up and gathered his things, deeply creasing the worry lines across her face. And she looked at me, her eyes filled with sadness, and said, "He isn't living here anymore."

I wasn't sure what I was expecting, but it definitely wasn't that. "What? We just broke up; what do you mean? How did he get a place so quickly?"

She exhaled through her nose, and instead of answering my questions, she simply told me his apartment number. He was still living in the same building. I walked to his front door and knocked.

When he opened the door, the reality I'd been building crashed down around me. The apartment behind him had a sofa, a TV on top of a TV stand, a bookshelf, and a dining table surrounded by tables. It was fully furnished, and beautifully put together.

174

"It's for Karen," he said. My breath quickened. I blinked to clear my vision. "She's coming to live with me."

I was dizzy with betrayal. I thought of the dimly lit and sparsely equipped apartment we'd been living in together for the past year. The mattress we shared was still on the floor, with no frame to support it. He'd always refused to invest in one with me and didn't spend a penny on other household essentials. I paid for it all. I always wondered what he was saving for. Now, I had my answer.

I couldn't believe how stupid I'd been. I questioned his spending, but he would never tell me and get upset, as it was none of my business. A part of me always hoped that maybe he was setting aside most of his money for Bruno's future, but I never dared to insist on questioning him, afraid of causing an unnecessary argument. But I should've known ever since the day he came home with a new car and didn't let me drive it while my car was falling apart at the seams. My car had broken doors and a sputtering engine, the car that drove our son around and allowed me to buy the food we ate, which he also never chipped in for. The signs had been in my face, dancing in front of me for years, and I willingly turned a blind eye.

Aleks grinned at the heartbreak written all over my face. He was merciless; he always enjoyed seeing me embarrassed and beamed with pride at being the cause of it. "I know what you're thinking," he said, readying himself to dig the knife deeper. "But look, you and I both know the truth here: Karen deserved it. You didn't. She comes from a good family. They have good morals and standards. You, you come from the trash."

"That's..." I stumbled over my words, trying to string together a sentence without crying. "That's not—that's not true."

"Oh, come on, you met her. Do you think you're better?"

"We have a *son* together."

"That doesn't mean you deserve it. You don't. You never did."

Everything became a blur, due to a mix of my tears and the fogginess that had settled on my brain. I always knew Aleks to be careless, but I didn't know he could be this *cruel*, and he was so unapologetic about it. I didn't know what to say. But there was nothing else to say, anyway. I was tired of fighting.

He made motions for me to come in and closed the door behind me; I sank to the floor right there in front of the door inside his apartment. I pulled my knees to my chest, hugging them as tightly as I could, and I cried like a child. I'd cried over Aleks a million times before in my life; I'd been crying over him since I'd met him, if I'm honest. He'd only ever caused me pain. But this time, something unlocked in my chest. I could see my life stretching out in front of me, and I saw it moving away, far away, from Aleks and the life he'd chosen to live. I cried and cried, and I was finally letting go of everything we'd been and could've been. Whatever it was, I didn't want to be that anymore. I didn't want any part in it.

I had no idea what would happen next. I had no idea that he and Karen would get married and have a loveless marriage for 15 years, a marriage of convenience above all else, at least in Aleks's eyes. I had no idea they'd have three kids or that he'd ruin her self-esteem like he did mine because maybe I would've warned her. I had no idea that Karen would call me later down the line and ask me if he'd done these terrible things to me that he was now doing to her, and I'd say that yes, he did. I had no idea that we'd become friends and stay friends after their divorce.

At that moment, as I cried, leaning against his front door, the only thing I knew for sure was that it was over. For good. And in all the misery he'd caused me, there was something to be grateful for. It was something to latch on to. It was hope.

I wiped my tears, got to my feet, and headed to work.

CHAPTER 37

The End of a Romantic, the Birth of an Atheist

I think that was when the romantic in me finally gave up. I thought Aleks had gotten rid of her a long time ago, but I felt colder than I ever had before in my life. Anything that had kept any semblance of true love alive in me had died the moment I closed Aleks's apartment door. There was no point in marrying for love, and I already knew that. It was why I'd stayed with Daniel for so long. But I lost focus when Aleks came back to trample all over my life again. It was time I got back on track.

I had a few goals in mind: become financially stable on my own, pay for my son's school, and marry an American to help me get my papers. I never saw myself stooping to that level—I always thought I'd marry for love. But all that had been thrown out the window along with Aleks's things. I couldn't be the fool anymore; I had to play it smart from then on, so I toughened up. The only love I had room for was my family. My son.

Another aspect of my life died at the same time. All the big dreams, illusions, or things that were not concrete or rational were also gone. And with included God. I remember I was crying, sitting on the floor in Aleks's apartment, and asking why God would allow me to go through all of these things. If there was a God, He had to be evil. It was easier for me to believe that He did not exist. I became an atheist.

I worked more hours than ever before, especially since Aleks still wasn't paying anything to help Bruno, but I still managed my life well to have quality time with Bruno. I had extra energy now since I didn't have to spend it all on Aleks anymore. A roommate moved into my apartment to lighten the load of rent. I was completely in the zone, dedicated to getting my life together and nothing—no one—else.

I ended up toughening myself up a bit too much and became a walking red flag myself. But of course, I figured this out after most of the mistakes had already been made.

I went to visit a friend in another town, an old one from Goiânia who had recently made the move to Florida. We hadn't been particularly close, but I was itching to connect with old friends, especially with girlfriends. I was trying to feel like a whole person again, in a life without Aleks.

While visiting her, I met Harvey—a somewhat typical American boy with a somewhat typical American lifestyle, and I wasn't as impressed as I always thought I would be. Harvey was kind and definitely charming, but I was immune. He couldn't sweep me off my feet, no matter how hard he tried. And he tried a lot. My feelings for him were similar to what I felt for Daniel: I ended up loving him, but I was never in love with him, no matter how much I knew it would be great if I did. So instead, I tried just as much as he did, in a different way.

There was one huge bonus to my efforts and to the American lifestyle: Harvey's family. They were incredibly welcoming and clearly tight-knit, and they didn't hesitate to open their arms to me. It was the family I'd always wanted and never had. So, I ignored whether or not I had real feelings for Harvey. I fell into them happily, accepting their warmth with gratitude. It was a nice contrast to the cold personality I'd adopted.

Harvey and I got married within two months of knowing each other. So, in other words, we didn't know each other at all. He liked me, and he meant well; that much was obvious. Although he knew of my baggage, he did not fully comprehend, nor did I know anything of his. It didn't help that I severely underestimated the weight he carried in his own world; familial trauma had a way of hunting you down, which I knew too well but couldn't imagine the way it affected Harvey. His family had moved to the US from Cuba, where they'd lost absolutely everything, but had managed to build a life slowly yet surely for themselves in Florida. This showed up in Harvey in the form of extreme paranoia and anxiety, to the point of neuroticism. Harvey was the youngest sibling of the family, and he had the biggest heart of all, but this also meant that he was wildly insecure and jealous, on top of everything else. It all meshed in a combination that drove me insane due to my lack of patience.

Every time I went to work, he'd be terrified that someone was going to kill me in the parking lot. He was suspicious of any unfamiliar interactions and was convinced that everybody was out to get us. We soon had a daughter together, Natalia, and he immediately projected the same fears onto her. He didn't trust anyone around our child. It was like this 24/7, and it drove me insane. Our fighting began quickly.

Harvey and I moved closer to my mother as I hoped to give her another chance at being a grandmother to Natalia. And I didn't want Harvey's family, no matter how much I loved them, to be the only family that Natalia knew. I hoped that she would wake up something in my mother, some maternal instinct that had never kicked in. But again, to no avail: she was still always too busy for her family.

After getting my American documents, thanks to Harvey, I got a job at a hotel nearby and was shocked that I got paid *less* than I did before. What was the point of doing things the right way if there were no rewards to be reaped? But I continued, not having any other choice, and over time, I got a different job as a teller at a bank. It wasn't a lot, of course, but it was an easier job than cleaning houses. Harvey and I both worked all the time and made enough to put Bruno and Natalia through school and take care of our family.

My financial life was finally, *finally* stable. I had long ago gotten rid of that terrible car, and I didn't have to worry about rent or groceries. I could almost breathe. Almost. But when one problem loosened its grip, another one swooped in. My relationship with Harvey was falling apart, but it had never really been good in the first place. Bruno was old enough to be able to tell, and Natalia would be soon enough. Instead of being the victim of familial trauma, I'd become the cause.

I decided to get out of it as soon as I could. It was for the better, and we both knew it. I moved to be closer to Eliza, who'd started her own daycare in her home. So, while Bruno was in school and I was at work, I'd support Eliza's newfound business by paying her fee and leaving Natalia with her for the day. She was the only person I trusted enough to help raise my children.

Aleks had already ruined my perception of romantic love, and now Harvey had ruined my perception of marriage, too. I didn't believe in it anymore, not even for its benefits. I started to let go of the idea that I'd ever settle down for love. More than anything, for the first time in my life, I wanted to have *fun*. I was twenty-four years old, and somehow, the only partying I'd ever done was in my early teens. How did adults have fun? How did moms have fun? How did *women* have fun? I'd become a mother while still in my girlhood and had given up any semblance of enjoyment or pleasure. It was time to rediscover it on my own terms.

CHAPTER 38

It is Time to Have Fun!

This was when I met Kat, or more like we re-met. She was another person I knew from Goiânia, from my time in Catholic school, and it was like she could sense my current desperation. I'd had enough of men holding me back in life. It was time for me to spend time with women who'd push me forward, and that was what Kat gave me…in a way I hadn't expected.

She had a big group of other Brazilian girlfriends who'd party every weekend and had lines of men for them around the block. They were all drop-dead gorgeous, and everyone could see it. I was quickly integrated into them, leaving Bruno and Natalia with their fathers on weekends to join the girls on whatever new escapade they'd planned. Sometimes, there weren't any plans at all, and we'd go wherever the night ended up taking us. In the beginning, I loved the excitement of it; I had barely lived for myself in the past few years, and I was making up for it now.

I started drinking again, and ironically enough, it made me feel like a teenager. My new friends would go beyond my limits, trying things like ecstasy and cocaine, things I was always too afraid to reach for, thankfully. I wanted to have fun without anxiety in any form, whether due to drugs or relationships. I'd been chasing things that made me miserable for my whole life, and now I just wanted a break.

They were a great form of escapism, mainly because their realities were so wildly different than mine. A friend of a friend, one of the girls who lived out of town, and I hadn't met yet, had a husband who was deported, forcing them both to move to Brazil together. Every couple of months, he'd send her to New York City to dance at some strip clubs, make money, and then come back, where they'd live off of the money until it ran out. They'd go back and forth like this.

Upon hearing that this infamous friend was coming back to the States, the girl group decided to make the trip over to New York. It would be my first time going, and I was ecstatic. We made our plans, I left the kids with their fathers, and we went.

Although I was excited about New York, it wasn't the only thing that sparked my joy about this adventure. It was the first time I could afford to travel with my own money, and I didn't have to worry about being able to provide. I could take a week off work and pay for the trip. It would be a little tight, but I could do it. It felt like the world was finally opening up for me, and a better life was within my reach for the first time.

The World Cup was happening in Japan that year, and everyone was watching, especially us Brazilians. But because of the different time zones, the games were always in the middle of the night. It was easy to find more of us in New York, friends of friends everywhere who had their own apartments in Manhattan. Every single night, we'd hop from bar to club around the city, head to someone's place to watch the game in a packed apartment, and go back to our hotel in the morning, where we'd sleep all day until it was time to do the same thing all over again.

My friends knew how to have the type of fun I was still figuring out. For most of the week, I was the only one who'd consistently gone back to the hotel every night while they tended to find someone to spend the night with. I tried it once that week because I felt I owed it to myself. I was always tied down to someone, pronouncing undying, undeserved loyalty, but now the only thing I wanted to commit myself to was my pledge to the single life. But the next morning, as I left the apartment of this guy I barely knew and would most likely never see again, I felt miserable. Wasn't this supposed to feel good? I couldn't understand how or why people do this. Unfortunately, this was not the last time this would happen. My lack of self-esteem drove me to other nights like this; I hated myself for that.

The week passed by quickly. Since we were a group of women, well-dressed and beautiful, we got into any club we wanted. I saw more celebrities than I expected. One night, we bumped into one of the lead actors from *Top Gun* and took a picture with him. I imagined what the folks in Goiânia would say if they knew, let alone the ones in Olímpia. I was living in the States, partying in New York with my friends, and meeting world-renowned actors. But as the time went on, something felt off.

The last night arrived, and we were once again watching the game at someone's apartment. I didn't know the owner, but I hadn't known the owner of any of the other apartments we'd stayed at. It quickly turned into a party, packed with more people than usual. Drinks were flowing, someone started passing around coke, and I eyed it curiously, watching as the next taker lined it up. When it was handed to me, I quickly passed it on to someone else, and one of my friends asked me if we should try. Music played louder and louder. Another of my friends passed out in a different room. I just wanted to watch the game.

I told someone—one of the girls, I don't remember which—that I was leaving, going back to the hotel. She said they were staying longer and asked me to stay with them, but I didn't. The game was over. The sun was starting to show up. There was nothing else to stay for.

I walked aimlessly around Manhattan. The sun was rising, reflecting on the windows of skyscrapers, painting the city in a golden hue. I thought of how some people called heaven the golden city, and I wondered if those people had ever seen New York at sunrise. I wondered if this was really what my life was supposed to be if I'd peaked. Most people would say I had—meeting celebrities at nightclubs and hotels in Manhattan, wasn't that what life was supposed to be about? And if it was, why wasn't I enjoying it as much as I thought I would? As much as I *wanted* to.

I got tired of walking. I waved over a cab, gave them the address to the hotel, and packed my things as soon as I arrived. But I couldn't shake off the thought that life had to be more than this.

CHAPTER 39

That is How we Met

I didn't stop spending time with these friends. But I began to find that there were days I wanted to go out on my own and choose my adventure. I'd inevitably meet people, get looped into groups of strangers, and dance the night away with them, trying to fill that same void I felt in Manhattan.

One night, I stood on the upper level of a lounge, looking down at the moving masses below. Were these people happy? Did they have the same void I did? How did they fill it? I knew what I really craved—to be loved unconditionally, a relationship, a truly loving relationship that would last. I wasn't even sure if I believed in those anymore. I began to sob in that lounge, unable to stop. I was chasing temporary highs with these friends, with these parties, and once it faded, I was all alone again.

My friend hosted a barbecue on a Sunday night. It might've been a birthday, but regardless of the event. I found myself drunkenly kissing a friend. I didn't know how it started, but I wasn't going to stop it either. I craved connection, and this was as far as I'd go to get it. I wasn't willing to put myself in a position where I'd get hurt again.

"We're going to that club later that has the Brazilian night," he told me, and I knew exactly what he was talking about. My friends and I would frequent it some Sundays. We agreed to meet each other there later.

Hours later, after the barbecue and after we girls had dressed up in our night attire, the guy I was kissing didn't show up. I found myself relieved. I was open to meeting him, but if I was honest, I didn't want things to go any further. He was a friend, and I wanted to keep it that way to avoid getting attached.

One of my friends immediately hit the dance floor and was pulled in by a man around our age. I watched, leaning against the bar with the rest of my friends. They moved fluidly and effortlessly, but the moves they did were simple enough. I always admired dancers since I was terrible at it myself. When I was tipsy enough, I could let loose, but otherwise, my movements were always stiff. But the way this guy danced made me think that I could keep up with him. In fact, I felt like I could actually be a good dancer if I was dancing with him.

I downed my drink and approached them. I knew my friend wouldn't mind if I cut in—she had a boyfriend and would dance with anyone. Sure enough, when she saw me approaching, she gave me a wide grin and took a step back. She always supported my flings, constantly trying to set me up with someone.

His back was turned to me, so I tapped him on the shoulder. He whirled around. He was taller than me and looked down at my face with a goofy smile, probably drunk. I gestured for him to lean down to my level, and he did, placing his ear close to my mouth so I could speak over the music: "Do you want to dance?"

He immediately put his arms around me and began to sway us, moving just as smoothly as he had before. I was immediately impressed; my stiffness had a tendency to be contagious, and I'd find myself stepping on my partner's toes and making us both trip over our feet. But this time, with him, his gracefulness reflected onto my steps. He made it easy to keep up with, just as I thought he would. We fit together perfectly; he was the dance partner I'd been looking for.

After a while of dancing, we both went to grab a drink with the rest of my friends, sweaty and breathless. A friend who wasn't usually with our group came with us that night, and she stood with her shoulders tensed, not making conversation with anyone. She looked around nervously, her fingers tapping the bar.

"Hey," I said, sidling in next to her. I searched her worried face. "Are you okay?"

"I think those guys are following me," she said, nodding towards the crowd. I glanced over. I couldn't tell who she was gesturing to; the place was packed.

"Oh, please, how can you even tell?" said one of our friends who'd overheard, vocalizing my exact thoughts. "Don't worry, I'm sure it's fine."

"No, I'm serious, I think my boyfriend sent them," she insisted. And then she sighed and stood up straighter, preparing herself. She stepped closer to our group so everyone could hear her better. I glanced over my shoulder and saw my dance partner still standing there. He was ordering a drink and didn't seem to be listening at all. "Look, trust me, someone's following me. Watch. I'm going to pretend to head toward the exit and then loop back around here. Pay attention and see if I'm being followed. It's two short guys; one of them is bald."

Before we could say anything else, she turned and pushed her way through the crowd, heading straight for the front door. I watched her closely, becoming increasingly nervous for her. She'd seemed more serious than I'd ever seen her. As she approached the exit, two men materialized behind her, one of them bald, just as she'd said. They followed her, always a few steps behind, doing their best to not be too obvious. I was impressed that she'd noticed them at all; they moved so discreetly amongst a crowded, dark room. It looked like a movie as if she were the target of a spy attack.

She looped back around and came straight back towards us. The men watched and fell back when they saw she was staying. She looked at us with wide eyes. "Did you see? Did you see them?"

I nodded stiffly. "Um…yeah."

"That was…creepy," another girl said, and everyone in our group vocalized their agreement.

"Okay, so, what do we do?" I asked her.

She looked back towards the crowd, where the men had already disappeared but were surely lying in wait. She gestured for us to come in closer, and we did, leaning in intently. "We're all going to move towards the main exit as a group, so it looks like we're all leaving. They probably have their eye on you guys, too, since we came together. When we get close to the door, we'll duck so we're covered by the crowd, and we'll stay down and head towards the back door. Once we get there, we *run*, okay? As fast as we can."

Everyone nodded, completely locked in, and put our plan into motion. We headed towards the front door just as she said, and when I looked behind me, I could see the same bald head illuminated by the lights. We got closer to the front door, and she ducked just as planned. We all followed suit. We moved as quickly as we could in our crouched positions towards the back door. We probably looked insane to anyone moving past us, and I could only imagine what was running through my dance partner's mind when I found him as we passed by the bar. I grabbed his arm and brought him to crouch down with me as we kept moving, which was even more difficult for him.

"What are you doing?" he asked, raising his voice to be heard over the music.

I smiled. I liked that he was crouched with me without even knowing why. "Come with me," I told him.

He smiled back and let me drag him away.

The girls in the front of the group pushed open the front door, one of them holding it open as we all made it through, and then we booked it. My dance partner kept pace with me for a while without asking questions until we were almost to our cars, and the girls began looking for their keys.

"Wait, wait, what are we doing? Why are we running?" he finally asked.

"I can't—I can't explain right now," I said, breathless. "But meet us...at the Brazilian pizza place...you know the one?"

He nodded. "Okay. Can I get your name first, at least?"

"Be there, and I'll tell you."

He rolled his eyes, but he wore a smile. "Fine. See you there."

I could hear footsteps, and I knew I had to go. I turned and ran toward the car the girls were piling into, this time hoping that maybe this guy would be there.

The pizzeria was open 24/7 as their main clientele consisted of club-goers, and being a Brazilian restaurant, they were especially busy on Sunday nights. We arrived, high on adrenaline, giddy at getting away from it. It really felt like a movie, and it was feeding my inner romantic. The car I was in was the first to arrive, but the rest of our group arrived shortly after. We all sat at a table, one that had become our usual, as the rest of us slowly piled in. A group of about 20 people showed up, and we pushed our tables and chairs closer together. The staff didn't mind; Brazilians always did this. They were used to it by now.

My dance partner showed up with the rest of the crowd. He walked right up to my spot and plopped down next to me. I felt just as electric with him as I had on the club floor. We caught the group up on our story of what just happened—the stalkers, the bald guy, running out the back door—leaving room for some extra dramatics because we loved to entertain a crowd.

At some point, I learned that my dance partner's name was Sebastian, and he was four years younger than me. I was immediately turned off by even the concept of potentially dating someone younger than me. I was 26, married and divorced, and had two kids. I'd had a fling with a younger guy before, and it ended poorly—he was immature, unable to handle the harsh reality of my life. I could tell that Sebastian was interested, possibly in something more, but I was only interested in the night. I'd wanted someone to dance with, and he'd given me that. So, when dawn approached, and we all walked out of the pizzeria, spilling out onto the sidewalk like a leak had sprung, and Sebastian leaned in to kiss me, I turned away.

"You're really, really fun," I told him, doing my best to be as kind but firm as possible. "But that's all for me."

"Oh, come on, you can't tell me I'm the only one who felt something here," he said with a smile. He was taking it well, at least. I'd gotten much worse reactions from men.

And he was right—I had felt something. But I couldn't let him know that. It'd just make things harder. I shrugged at him. "Sorry. But if you ever need someone to dance with, you know who to call."

"So I can call you?"

I smiled and shook my head. "Just for a night out. I'll see you around."

That was how I met my future husband.

CHAPTER 40

The Pot and the Kettle

I went to work as usual the next day, despite running on just a few hours of sleep. I'd recently been promoted to Personal Banker, which at least meant I didn't need to interact with people as much as I did when I was still a teller. I was generally a social person, but not when I was hungover after a long night out.

The day went on as usual until I received a phone call in my office, and I recognized the voice on the other end of the line.

"Good morning!" Sebastian said cheerily. "When's our next date?"

I couldn't help but laugh at his sunny cadence. "Good morning to you, too, but I don't remember ever having a first date."

"Sure you do. Last night, running from the bald guy? Great first date, by the way."

I ignored that. "Sebastian, we talked about this last night."

"I remember *you* talking, and I just kind of listened," he joked again, but then his tone became more genuine. "Let me take you out. For real."

"I'm sorry, but I really can't," I said. "I'm not dating right now?"

"How about later? Like, this afternoon?"

191

"Bye, Sebastian."

"Bye, Cris. Same time tomorrow?"

I hung up, trying to stop a smile from spreading on my face. I was used to persuasive guys, but there was something different about him. This time, a part of me *wanted* the persuasion. Beneath my outer defenses, I wanted to go out with him, but how could I be sure that it would be *okay* to date again? That things would work out this time. The uncertainty terrified me. I needed to be in control of my life, and dating was so out of my control.

Sure enough, when he really did call at the same time the next day, just like he'd said. He'd call to chat, but ultimately to try to convince me to go on a date with him. "Look, you're beautiful, and *so* interesting and fun," he said. "I'd really love to get to know you more."

I thought it was a waste of time, and I tried to convince him of that, too. I didn't mention my kids or anything about my personal life—I just said that we were too different and I wasn't dating. So I was shocked when he called again on Thursday that week, for the fourth day in a row, and immediately said, "So, what's the deal? Why don't you want to go out, *really?* You think I care that you have three kids?"

Unable to hold it back this time, I burst out laughing. "*Three* kids?" I said between giggles. "I have *two*. Who even told you that?"

"Two, three, same thing."

"Well, it's not—"

"No, no, it's not," he hurried to say, backtracking. "I mean, you know what I mean, it's not the same thing, but to me, it's the same—like, it's not a problem, for me, if we—if you want to—go out."

I laughed again at his rambling. "Look, I'm just saying it's something for you to think about. You're young; I don't want to complicate things. If we go out and dance, that's fine, but I don't think you really want to go further than that."

"First of all, I'm not that much younger than you," he replied. "Second of all, I've had all week to think about it, and if I'm still calling you, I'm obviously fine with it. And lastly, I *do* want to go further than that. I'm not afraid of anything or your kids, and I really, *really* want to go out with you. So, what are you doing tonight?"

I felt my heart thump in my chest.

We went out that same night to a birthday party for one of his close friends, a guy named Tim. I felt a bit put on the spot—who took a first date to your closest friend's birthday, anyway? He knew more people than I did, but most of our friends ran in the same group, so this alleviated some of the pressure I was feeling. I was cautious about not presenting ourselves as a "couple"—we were just hanging out semi-romantically.

People drank and smoked, as usual. Sebastian had a couple of beers, and I partook as well. Someone was passing around a weed joint, and it eventually made its way to Sebastian and me. I held it momentarily, and I was going to take a puff. But Sebastian nodded and gave me a small smile.

"I don't really like girls who do drugs or smoke, so," he shrugged. It was a simple statement that shouldn't have meant much, but for some reason, we *connected* for the first time. I did not feel like he was trying to control me, but that he wanted a future with me. I never even thought about smoking again, nor did Sebastian and I ever separate.

This didn't mean that my relationship issues were suddenly solved—far from it. My trust issues were still off the charts, and I didn't expect Sebastian to fix that overnight, nor did I want him to. I refused to call it a relationship and kept my definition of a semi-romantic hangout. We'd keep spending time together while it suited us both, but when it ended—and I was sure it would, sooner or later—I wouldn't push things any further. I wouldn't ask him to stay or pine after him.

I'd never witnessed a healthy, lasting relationship. My parents divorced when I was young, and Madonna and my Father were the definition of a toxic relationship, Aleks's parents seemed perfect on the surface level, but they fell apart quickly as well. I'd been divorced, had broken up with every guy I'd ever loved, and had been betrayed more times than I could count. Nothing lasted forever, and this *definitely* wouldn't.

But the longer that our hangouts went on, the more difficult it became to imagine life without him. It was difficult to not get attached to him, nearly impossible. He was attractive, funny, and I got along with him more than I had with any other boyfriend or any person in my entire life. We could talk about anything; he got along well with my kids. We were like a pot and kettle, in both good and bad ways.

I loved going out to drink and dance with friends, and he loved it even more. Whenever we wanted a night out, I'd hire a babysitter, and we'd be gone until the sun rose. Our friend group quickly combined, and we even developed a schedule for the best places to go each night. Sundays and Wednesdays were our favorites— on Sundays, we'd go to the club that had a Brazilian night, like on the night that we'd first met; on Wednesdays, a local bar sold a pitcher of beer and Jell-O shots for a dollar each, and they'd blast Bob Marley all night. I never saw a girl need to pull out their wallet at that place— the moment a cup was empty, a man would come along and pay for another. Being just a dollar, it was the perfect place to get drunk and find someone to go home with. I had already frequented this place before meeting Sebastian, but now it was even more.

Our friend groups tied themselves together, maybe even a little too tightly at times. We did absolutely everything together. Folks started dating each other; some of them just messing around and others moving in together, sometimes both simultaneously. Eventually, Sebastian and I followed suit. We'd been in this relationship, although I was still hesitant to call it that, for a few short months when he wanted to move out from his roommate's place. He was apartment-hunting, and my roommates had recently moved out as well. I figured that it was the most convenient thing to do, and my kids liked him anyway—why not move in together?

I tried to treat this milestone a lot more casually than I had with Aleks. Things would always complicate themselves if I sped things up or made a big deal out of things. Sebastian moving in was out of convenience, I told myself, and *nothing more*. And frankly, it didn't change our relationship much either; he already slept over enough as it was.

CHAPTER 41

Friday Night Hangouts

Before I met Sebastian, his friend group started a routine. The parents of a couple of his friends, a brother, and a sister, invited their whole group of friends to meet at their houses on Friday nights. Just a casual hangout and food. When I met Sebastian, I started going to these Friday night meetings. We were a group of Brazilian immigrants, the majority here without our families. We were on our own, and having some semblance of a family meant more to us than they could imagine.

We quickly became comfortable with these loving parents, calling them Mamas and Pops. They took us in, practically adopted us. It became expected, our meeting point, every Friday night: "I'll see you at Ellen's," otherwise known as Mamas. We'd feast on those nights as they'd make us far more food than we needed despite being a group of around twenty young adults. We'd sit in a circle and pass around plates of food while Mamas and Pops would give us conversation prompts, the usual one being, "Talk about something good." Happy emotions we'd felt lately, what we're up to, what's something *good* in your life. More often than not, we'd tell Ellen and her husband that *they* were something good in our lives. They gave us a family when we forgot what it felt like to have one.

Our routines were the same every weekend: meet at Ellen's around eight o'clock on Friday, leave for the club at ten or eleven o'clock, party the night away, and go our separate ways on Saturday mornings since some of us had work. I had a shift every now and then at the bank since we were on rotation on weekends, and Sebastian regularly worked Saturday mornings. But once it was nightfall, we'd go to the club again.

Sundays were my favorite. It was an all-day party. We'd go to the beach and have a barbecue, cheering with our beers in celebration of absolutely nothing, and spend the whole day drunk and tanning in the hot Florida sun. Then we'd go get dressed and go to the Brazilian-themed club night we were all anticipating, dance until our feet hurt, and stop at the Brazilian pizzeria before going home. Weekend after weekend, our days and nights turned into months. And despite the melancholy I'd felt in Manhattan, this was different. I still had an emptiness in me that I couldn't seem to fill, but Sebastian was good at distracting me from it, filling up some of the gaps himself. I was far from whole, but I felt a little more complete with him, though I'd never admit it.

CHAPTER 42

I Was Forced into a Bible Study

Things began to change when Eliza called me. She didn't have a daycare at her home anymore but was instead a live-in nanny at someone's house. I'd long ago hired a different babysitter, feeling guilty for relying on Eliza for so long when she'd done so much, too much, for me over the past decade. But we always stayed in touch; she was the closest mother figure that I had, who loved me healthily and wholly.

We exchanged pleasantries and made small talk—"How are you? How's Bruno? I miss him. How's that boy you're seeing?"—before she dove into what the call was really about. "I've been doing Bible studies," she told me. "At Aleks' home."

She was careful not to mention Karen to me, even after all this time, and I was still grateful for it. I'd heard through the grapevine that they were still living together, but I had no desire to talk about it, and she knew that.

"The woman I'm studying with thinks I should find a new place to do them, and I agree," she continued. "So, I was wondering if I could do them in your home. At Aleks house is just not working, and I'd love to see Bruno more often, too."

I hesitated. There'd been a recent trend I'd noticed in Brazilian immigrants who moved to the States. They'd move here, typically Catholics or not religious, and for one reason or another would end up converting to evangelicals. I joked to Sebastian that it was like a virus, a plague.

There was a woman who lived in my apartment building who'd regularly stop me to tell me to change my lifestyle. Not only about my partying habits, but even my *groceries*. She'd point to whatever bag I was holding and say, "That bar code on your lemons? It's the mark of the *beast*. Every barcode has 666 on it; did you know that?" She'd go on and on about how she was praying for Eminem, the rapper, to convert to Christianity because her husband was a huge fan of Eminem, and it was the only way he'd convert. It took all of my will not to laugh in her face, and she quickly became symbolic, to me, of what I imagined all these converts to act like.

I knew that Eliza was still religious, but after my Catholic upbringing and everything I'd been through, I found it difficult to believe in God. Not just difficult, *impossible*. I'd concluded that God didn't exist years before and became stubborn about it. I couldn't believe that a supposedly loving God would let so much evil happen in the world, and I'd talk about it to anyone who'd ask my opinion on the subject. I thought believing in God was stupid, religion was stupid, and especially the Bible was stupid. Only uneducated, naive people would believe in this Book written thousands of years ago, by humans. There was a story of people worshiping a golden calf in the Bible, and I didn't see how Christians or Catholics were any different than that. The whole thing was a conspiracy theory in my eyes. Sebastian would say that my catchphrase was, "We're born, grow, multiply, get old, and die, and to not feel that life is completely meaningless, we made up a god." I suppose I was a bit nihilistic. I was irritated by the conversion trend and didn't want to see it happening to any of my friends, *especially* not Eliza, not after everything she'd done for me. So I let her use my apartment,

200 | Broken by Love: The Story of an Atheist Turned Pastor

and even told her I'd join in for some. I didn't tell her that I had no interest in religion but would actually be eavesdropping in order to keep an eye out for her.

After our conversation, Eliza started coming over every Wednesday for one-on-one Bible studies with one of her local church leaders, a woman who always wore modest clothing, usually a skirt, and introduced herself as Mabel. I decided off the bat that I didn't trust her. I was suspicious of anything religious, and that included her. I planned to go out on Wednesday evenings to avoid hearing their conversations, but then I'd become anxious about what Mabel might be teaching Eliza in my apartment and found myself staying around and then venting to Sebastian. Was she being manipulated? Did she actually believe in this stuff? So I started sticking around more often, busying myself in the kitchen while they sat in the living room, always close enough to hear but not so close that they'd think of including me.

Still, Eliza always tried her best to have me join. She was gently persistent, a gentle nudge in a different direction. She'd ask just once or twice if I wanted to sit with them that day, just to listen in, and I wouldn't have to say a word. Of course, with my stubbornness and the constant reminder of the fanatic who lived in my building, I always declined. But as the weeks went by, I found myself chiming in whenever a ridiculous claim was made. I didn't see it as any different from the spirits my Mom used to believe in, or the cup game that my friends would play.

Mabel always kept her composure when I went against her word, or God's Word, as she saw it. But it was harder for me to keep my cool, especially when I felt that I was defending Eliza. Sometimes, Sebastian would be around when we went head-to-head, snickering to himself while he grabbed a snack. I saw Mabel and me as being on opposite sides—she believed in fairytales, and I believed in what I could see, in the common knowledge that the world held, history, and proven facts of science.

"What about evolution?" I asked during one of her first visits. She'd been covering the early books of the Bible, and I thought the creation belief was the most ridiculous biblical concept. Yeah, sure, like the Earth was made in seven days. I couldn't understand why people believed it.

"Well, what about evolution?" she replied patiently.

"I mean, there's a lot of evidence backing it up. It makes way more sense."

"Evolution doesn't necessarily cancel out creation," she pointed out. "Besides, evolution is still just a theory, the same way creation is. They're two different theories, neither of them proven, both with evidence to back them up."

What proof could there possibly be for a theory as outlandish as creation? But I didn't want to push too much when this was for Eliza, not for me. Besides, whenever I tried to argue, she'd often agree with me and even use whatever facts I spewed out to support her own claim. This frustrated me immensely at first, but then it began to draw me in. Mabel seemed to have an answer for everything, and I was fascinated.

I brought it up on the next Friday at Ellen's house, sharing my newfound interest with my friends. "It's bizarre how the things she talks about, in the Bible, actually line up with history," I told them. "It kind of makes sense, sometimes. I thought it was all made up."

They teased me at first, saying I was beginning to sound like those fanatics I hated so much. But as the conversation went on, I could tell they were just as intrigued as I was. "Why don't we invite her over?" Ellen suggested as she brought another plate of snacks for us. "I go to church with her. She's really smart. Seems like it would be an interesting conversation."

"I don't know if I need an existential talk before going to the club," someone joked, and we all laughed.

I shrugged and said, "Well, why not? I mean, I need you guys to tell me if I'm crazy for almost believing her."

We agreed to invite her the next Friday night as we headed out the door on our way to order a round of shots to start off the night. A week later, when Mabel showed up, I was determined not to let her presence change anything. It was just an added ritual to our usual night out, and she'd been invited out of pure curiosity. I refused to let it become anything more than that.

We piled into Ellen's small apartment like always, the same snacks she'd make for us, the same group of friends. But this time, we adjusted ourselves into a circle in the living room, sitting on the available couches and dropping to the floor when we ran out of seats. Mabel stood in front and began her spiel, a different story or biblical topic every week. I covered up my smugness whenever a friend spoke up to challenge something she said, igniting a passionate debate. I felt some pride at the idea that we might be a challenging group for her—a bunch of folks in their 20s, loud as ever, opinionated, and confident in speaking up about it. But I'd be lying if I said that she wasn't a challenge for us, too.

CHAPTER 43

Beach, Beer, and Bible

My friends and I had all long ago indoctrinated ourselves into the hook-up culture that permeated our generation, and this was no secret to Mabel or Ellen. Oftentimes, Ellen's house would be packed with over 50 people as we brought in new friends or flings. One time, we had a whopping total of 105 people, and we had to pile onto each other's laps for there to be enough room. Our lifestyles were rarely brought up, but when Mabel started talking about healthy relationships according to the Bible, the tension in the room was palpable.

"It seems kind of prude, doesn't it?" someone asked when Mabel talked about celibacy, prompting snickers from around the room. He'd said what we'd all been thinking.

"Think of it more as protecting yourself," she replied, calm as always. "It's not supposed to be prude, nor is sex supposed to be shameful. It's about saving yourself for someone, making it special for both of you. Sex isn't supposed to be meaningless; it's supposed to be kept for the right person in your life."

I didn't agree with everything Mabel said, frankly, but there was a little something that rang true in her words. About that someone special, the one thing I've always wanted to have in my own life.

Mabel's life lessons started to change others in our friend group, too, although you wouldn't be able to tell on a surface level. We still partied regularly and kept our usual schedules, but our conversations were completely different than what they used to be. While we lounged with our beers on the beach, we debated theological concepts, taking sides, and were passionate about our stance.

"But so, what if Constantine changed the Sabbath or whatever?" Geoff argued, another one of Sebastian's closest friends. He was in his usual uniform: baggy cargo shorts, shirtless, cold beer in hand, his long hair cascading down his shoulders and still wet from his dip in the ocean. His eyes were still somewhat red from the weed he'd smoked earlier. He handed me a beer from the cooler as he spoke. "Like, dude, what was the point of even doing that?"

"Okay, don't judge me, but I *did* read a biography on Constantine after Mabel talked about that," I said as I grabbed the beer, immediately met with a groan from Geoff.

"Sebastian, are you hearing this?" he asked my unresponsive boyfriend, who was lying on his towel with his eyes closed, his beer planted in the sand as a makeshift cupholder. "Like, come on, man, you're *studying* this now?"

"No, listen, listen," I laughed. I knew how ridiculous it sounded. "Look, Bruno had to do a research project in the library, so I just went with him and decided to do some reading while I was there. I needed something to do! Can you open this, by the way? I don't have an opener."

I handed my beer back to him as he grabbed his bottle opener keychain with his free hand. "Okay, whatever, what did you learn?" He popped the bottle open. "Did you want lime with this?"

I shook my head, and he handed the beer back to me. "Well, basically, everything Mabel said was true," I said. "Like the Bible aside, she actually backed it up with real stuff. I don't know why; I just didn't expect that—"

"But why does it *matter*?" Geoff asked. "Why does any of it matter? Sure, she was right about Constantine, but so what?"

"I don't know, I always thought that the Bible was, like, its own separate thing that couldn't apply to real-life history. I thought it was made up; you know? I didn't think there was anything real at all in there."

"Nah, I don't think it's that serious, dude," he replied. "Like, it's cool and all that maybe some of that stuff actually happened. But it doesn't mean they're right about *everything*."

I took a swig of my beer while Geoff turned to pestering Sebastian on a different topic. I hated to admit it, but my worldview had shifted entirely. I pushed it away as much as I could, but it came through in my personality. Thoughts control actions, and everything is different now, whether I want it to be or not.

CHAPTER 44

The Epiphany

Mabel had been giving Bible studies on Fridays for a few weeks when Sebastian and I fought. I don't remember what it was about, but it was bad enough that I cried on my way to work that morning. Is this the time the shoe drops, like in all my relationships? I'd begun to feel more convinced that there was some truth to Mabel's claims, and although I held myself back, I could tell that it was starting to change me.

Still, I felt disappointed with my life. That feeling I had in Manhattan followed me everywhere I went, and Sebastian couldn't fill that missing piece for me anymore. I liked him a lot. I started falling for him, but I still couldn't bring myself to feel safe enough. Obviously, we cared for each other, but I didn't know how to cope with a serious relationship. What would that mean for me after everything I'd been through?

I found myself praying as I drove. It happened naturally, without realizing I was doing it at first. I had to figure out why none of my relationships worked out, why it always went down the drain. Was it me? Was I the common factor in all these failed attempts at love? I needed answers. I *deserved* answers.

An epiphany hit me; unlike anything I'd ever felt before. I'd become more open to maybe accepting the idea that God existed, but the idea of God being able to speak to anyone still seemed ridiculous to me. I wouldn't have believed it was possible if it hadn't happened to me at that moment. A still, small voice in my head told me that until I had Him—God—in my life, none of my relationships would last.

I saw a film of my entire life pass in front of me, like a vision. All the suffering, the mistakes, the attempted and failed relationships, everything. And for the first time, I could see all the times that God had been looking out for me. The time I tried to play the cup game but couldn't. When I was lost in the middle of Brasília, I miraculously called the right number. All the time, I'd stumble through the dark streets alone, drunk after a club in the middle of the night by myself, and I never had any trouble. Every encounter that I almost could've had with the occult was because of my family's ties to it.

I remembered how my parents came to choose my name. They told me that they were torn between naming me after two famous witches that they regularly saw on television at the time. But in the middle of their debate, a plastic bag with my name stamped on it fell on the floor: Cristiane. It was a common name in Brazil, but it felt chosen.

God had always been preparing me for the work he wanted me to do. I went from being named after witches to Cristiane. A name originated from Christian origins, follower of Christ.

I knew right then and there, with a certainty I'd never had about anything else, that I needed God. I needed to live life with a purpose, and I couldn't fight the faith that had taken hold of me. It was time to change, for real. I was tired of handing myself over to men who never had my best interests at heart. I had to save myself for the right one—even if it wasn't Sebastian.

I called Sebastian as soon as I got back home; I never made it to work and told him to meet me at home on his lunch break.

208 | Broken by Love: The Story of an Atheist Turned Pastor

I anxiously waited for him there and to get the conversation over with. I knew what I needed to do, but I was dreading it. He walked in, and I was surprised to see a coworker of his from the construction site trailing shyly behind. I looked at Sebastian in question, but I would not allow anything to deter me.

Not in the mood to argue more than we already were, I pulled Sebastian into our bedroom. Soon to become *his* bedroom. I wrung my hands together and gave him my spiel in one breath: "I'm not going to have sex with you anymore at all because I decided to wait till marriage from now on. It's just something I need to do for my relationship with myself and, well, with God. So, I'm going to sleep in my kids' room; you can sleep in the bedroom, and if you want to break up with me because of that, then that's up to you, but this is how it's going to be from now on. I've made up my mind and you can't change it."

Sebastian blinked at me, an amused expression on his face. "Are you done?"

"Yes."

"Cris, you sound insane."

I sighed. I expected that reaction.

"Like, actually," he continued. "You used to *hate* all this stuff, and now you're making a complete 180. Does that not seem crazy to you? You sound like that lady in the hall that you hate."

"Okay, she's a little crazier than me—"

"Not by much." He shook his head, and I could tell he was serious. "Not anymore. Our relationship has been going great; why ruin it with this?"

"I'm not *ruining* it; I'm actually trying to give us a chance of something real."

He scoffed. "Look, I always supported you in pursuing this, in going to the Bible studies, but this is ridiculous. You're becoming another fanatic, and it's all because of Mabel!"

"Maybe, maybe not. But I'm not changing my mind."

He stared at me, shocked, but I held my ground. Finally, he shook his head again and walked out of the bedroom. I heard the front door slam as he left.

Looking back, maybe it was a bit extreme. I didn't need to go to that extent, but it was what I felt called to do at the time. It helped me get my life together, but most importantly it was the beginning of my healing process and rebuilding of self-worth.

But at that moment, once Sebastian had left the apartment, I began to question myself. What would I do if he actually left? I hated the current bank I worked at—they were a different chain than the bank I'd previously worked at—and had put in my two weeks recently. My last day was coming up, and there was no backup job in sight. I still had my kids to raise. Anxiety hit me like a ton of bricks, and I reached for my phone to call Sebastian. I needed to apologize and take it all back. But right as I grabbed my phone, it started ringing: Mabel was calling. I answered.

"Hey, I wanted to check in on you," she told me. "How are you doing?"

"Well, uh, not so great right now," I said and told her everything that had just happened. My epiphany, the conviction of it, and Sebastian's reaction. "I was about to call him back and say never mind—"

"I don't think you should," she cut me off. "Don't you see that everything is finally starting to fall into place? If you go back on it, then what makes you different from any of the other girls he's met at clubs?"

I cringed at the idea. I didn't like her perspective, but a part of me worried. *Was* there a difference between me and those girls? We'd moved pretty fast in our relationship; what if he never valued me?

Still, it didn't sit right with me that people always shamed women for who they slept with, yet never looked down on men for the same thing. I felt convicted with the truth of God, but not purity culture; it was always unfair and devalued women.

I knew that I didn't agree with it, but despite how good my relationship with Sebastian was, I'd been through so much that my self-esteem still told me I was only good for quick hook-ups. I didn't believe that virginity was tied to value, nor did I believe that everyone needed to go on a journey of abstinence—but it was one that *I* wanted to go on, for myself. One of the Bible stories that most drove my conversion was the one of Mary Magdalene. I understood how she felt when she knelt in front of Jesus, wiping his feet with her hair. I understood how difficult it was for her to find value in herself again. Sometimes, I felt we were the same person. I needed a cleanse from men, from everything. I needed a fresh start.

After I hung up with Mabel, I began to dial Sebastian's number when a call from Ellen came through. I sighed with relief upon seeing her name. I knew she'd have a wise word of comfort for me. I answered the phone and gave her the rundown again, including what Mabel had said, afraid that my voice might go hoarse from all the talking I was doing.

"I know it's scary," Ellen told me in her gentle, motherly voice. "But you got this feeling for a reason. You felt God speaking to you for a reason. If Sebastian really wants a future with you, and I think he does, then he'll understand. Just give him time."

So I did. Or at least, that's what I intended to do. The next day, Sebastian began packing his things, and I didn't stop him. The day after, when we'd both gotten home from work, he asked me to go to the beach. The sun was setting soon. He said he wanted to talk while we were there. He hadn't touched any of his things and hadn't continued packing since yesterday. It seemed like a romantic gesture, but I didn't want to get my hopes up. Sebastian wasn't much of a romantic, and I felt certain that he was going to break up with me for good on the beach. Still, we went.

As we walked, barefoot in the warm sand, the tide washing over our legs as it ebbed and flowed, Sebastian stumbled over his words as he tried to form a coherent thought. I waited, patiently, for him to gather himself so we could discuss what I thought was the inevitable: an impending breakup.

"I don't want to marry until I'm in my 30s," he finally said. "I'm only 22. You're only 26. We're so young, you know? I don't want to rush anything."

"I'm not trying to rush anything," I said.

"No, I know, I know that." He furrowed his brows, his internal struggle showing clearly on his face. "But Cris, to be completely honest with you...I know it's been a few short months, but I really believe you could be the one."

I almost froze in my steps. He'd told me he loved me before, but I'd never heard him say it like that. I wasn't sure how I felt about it. Was there such a thing as a single great love in someone's life? As soulmates? I had given up on that believe a long time ago. If there was, then I had to admit that I felt the same way about him. Which was why I felt a glimmer of hope at his confession.

"I'm just worried now," he went on, continuing at our slow pace. "About our relationship. I don't want it to, you know, get messed up just because of some fanatics."

Broken by Love: The Story of an Atheist Turned Pastor

I sighed, the hope in me dimming. "Sebastian—"

"It's really okay if you're religious now, I don't mind that at all," he said, stopping us in our tracks. The sun had almost fully set now, the sky colored in purple and orange. "I grew up Catholic, I believe in God, I just never practiced it. And it's fine if you want to follow your convictions, I actually fully support that. But I don't want it to change *us*. What we have."

"If you support my convictions," I said, "then you should understand that means that things will change. Things *have* to change."

He sighed and looked towards the horizon, the sun slipping behind the waves, its last golden lights fading into the evening. "I know. I just don't want them to."

The sunset. We left the beach and went home in silence.

CHAPTER 45

The Proposal

It was Father's Day that weekend, and since most of us didn't have any family living nearby, we decided to celebrate Mamas and Pops with a big brunch at a nearby restaurant. They truly did feel like our adoptive parents at that point, healthier than any family dynamic I'd ever had. I was beyond grateful to them and the life they'd helped me build.

My children were visiting their dads, leaving Sebastian and me alone as we got ready together that morning. We hadn't spoken much that morning, and I could tell that our relationship was hanging by a thread. I didn't know how to show up with everyone today, to smile and laugh and celebrate, when there was so much weighing on my head and heart. I knew I was going in the right direction, but I didn't know if Sebastian was willing to walk the same path with me.

When he went to take a shower, I found myself kneeling by my bed in prayer for the first time. I remembered rediscovering prayer when I was so young, lost in Brasília after getting kicked out of Adrian's apartment. How different this prayer was from the one I'd prayed back then. How many more things I'd lived through since then. Sometimes, I didn't know how I was still standing. But it'd all led me here, with Sebastian and my two kids and my wonderful newfound family in Florida. It had to be for a reason.

Something touched my foot then. *Grabbed* my foot, actually. I jumped, confused, and opened my eyes to see Sebastian sprawled across the floor behind me, still wet from his shower and wrapped in his towel, grabbing my foot teasingly.

He gave me a goofy grin. "You know, you could've given me a warning if you wanted to go cold turkey on our relationship," he joked.

We laughed. It was ridiculous—this, us, the whole situation. Everything. We both knew it, and everything changed with that knowledge. Sebastian had lightened up; I had, too. I didn't know what was going to happen next in our relationship, but I had a feeling we weren't going to break up after all. We were going to be okay.

Everyone was talking vividly—wide mouths, expressive hands, talking over one another and all at the same time—and although I couldn't hear a thing as we walked up to the entrance, I knew exactly what they were talking about.

The restaurant had enormous windows, giving us clear visual access to its dining room, where all of our friends had already gathered along with Mamas and Pops. Sebastian and I were the last to arrive, and I couldn't blame them for taking advantage of our absence to speculate about what would happen next in our relationship. I probably would've done the same if I were on the outside looking in. As soon as Sebastian opened the restaurant door, their voices floated over to us, confirming my suspicions.

"I think they're gonna break up," I heard a male voice say. "Cris is going too far."

"What, for not wanting to have sex?" A girl replied. "Don't be stupid."

"It's not just about the *sex*; it's about the *intention*. Like, sex is first, and then what? It changes the whole relationship dynamic."

"And maybe that's a good thing. Maybe they're growing up, which I know is hard for you to imagine."

Voices overlapped, but it was clear that the girls were defending me while the boys defended Sebastian. Sebastian gave me a glance and I rolled my eyes, shaking my head at it all when I heard a distinct voice above the rest.

"I think Cris is doing the right thing," Ellen said, and the rest of the table quieted. "You're right, she is growing up, but so are all of you. She's making this decision to give their relationship a real chance, and she deserves to do that."

Chatter ensued again as soon as she finished talking, but not for long. One of them noticed us and all their heads turned in our direction, dead quiet. Sebastian stormed up to the table so quickly that I trailed slightly behind, surprised by his sudden determination. He was walking like he was on a mission. What had gotten into him?

He reached the head of the table and slammed his hand on it to get everyone's attention, which was unnecessary since they were already staring at us enough as it was. I stayed behind him, dumbfounded and slightly embarrassed. Everyone waited for his next move.

"The woman decided to go on strike," he announced, "we're getting married."

Stunned silence ensued for a moment more before erupting into cheers and congratulations. I laughed as my friends jumped up from their seats to hug me, relief, confusion, and shock flooding my system. Through the chaos, Sebastian reached for my hand, excitement, and question in his eyes.

"Sebastian, what...?" I couldn't figure out how to finish my question, but he understood.

"Cris, I always wanted to marry you," he said. "I didn't think it'd be so soon, but it was always the plan. And I always believed in God; you just, well, scared me with the sudden extremeness. But if you're serious, and I'm serious about you, then, well, I wanna be serious together."

It was an absurd proposal, and yet made the most sense for the rollercoaster that our relationship had been. It was the end of an era, and the beginning of our new life together. I nodded, ecstatic, and he kissed me. Our friends cheered even louder.

CHAPTER 46

Changes Started Happening

The changes that had been planted through all our Bible studies began to show results soon after. Directly after Sebastian's proposal, we all sat down to eat, and teasing ensued, naturally. Most of the men at the table started turning to their girlfriends, saying, "Don't get any ideas!" But Sebastian and I were enveloped in bliss, and nothing could push through it.

Still, I couldn't help but notice Geoff sitting quietly next to his girlfriend, staring down at the table, seemingly lost in thought. I'd never seen him like that before—he was usually so loud, and teasing was in his nature. It was weird for the jokes to be coming from everyone else but him. I briefly wondered if he was just high again, but he was never good at covering it up whenever he was.

He wasn't the only one who decided to go sober that day. When the waiter came by to ask what everyone wanted to drink, almost everyone ordered their usual beers, but Sebastian hesitated. It was the first time I'd ever seen him not jump at a drink. He could hold his liquor pretty well and was known as one of the bigger drinkers in the group. So, when he ordered a water, looks of confusion and surprise were shared around the table.

Once the waiter left, Luke was the first to say, "I've *never* seen you order water. At least not without another drink on the side."

Sebastian sighed and said, "I don't drink anymore." He made that decision right there and then and never went back.

Gasps were heard around our table. It was a dramatic reaction for sure, but Sebastian was a consistent guy through and through. Up until today, he'd been a heavy drinker who wanted to get married in his 30s. And now he was engaged and going sober.

"Are you sure about this?" I asked him.

He looked down at me with a smile, his easy confidence melting me. "I am, actually. I'm sure about a lot of things today. Time to try something new, you know?"

His effortless conviction became contagious within our group. A few days later, Geoff told Sebastian and I that he'd decided to be abstinent as well until they decided to marry.

"We're gonna keep living together and all that," he said. "Like, we have a life together, and I don't want to give all that up, man. But I don't know, I guess I'm pulling a Cris." He chuckled to himself. "What's funny is that she's the one pulling a Sebastian—she's not dumping me or anything, but she's having a hard time adjusting to abstinence."

Our lives remained somewhat the same—Friday nights at Ellen's followed up by clubbing, Sundays spent lounging on the beach—but the shift this time was noticeable. Sebastian and I stopped drinking, although we continued going out, and it was strange to see us become somewhat pioneers of the group. Slowly, our influence trickled to the rest of them. Others stopped drinking and stopped smoking. Six other couples in our friend group went abstinent. Eventually, we all decided to go to church together and try it out.

For the first time, the hole in my heart began to fill.

CHAPTER 47

The Wedding

I'd never been in a limo before and certainly never expected to be in one for my wedding. But there it was, pulling up in front of my house, just two short months after Sebastian had proposed to me in front of all our friends. Some of those same friends gathered around me as we watched the long, sleek car pull up, giddy in their matching red dresses. I wondered if any of us could've guessed that we'd end up here ten months after I first met Sebastian at that club, running away from complete strangers. My face was sore from smiling, but I couldn't stop.

A church member who worked at a limousine company was kind enough to donate one for us to use in our wedding, complete with a driver. We were on a tight budget, but our local church had been so happy for us that we had a slew of volunteers to handle decorations, music, and even a donated timeshare in Orlando for our honeymoon. It was better than I ever imagined, Sebastian included.

I held my bouquet of red roses in my lap as we drove towards the church, music blasting around us in the limo, all the women talking and laughing around me. I smiled down at my beautiful dress, feeling confident in myself, something I was still getting used to. The past two months, amongst the chaos of wedding preparations, I'd been rebuilding myself. I'd never taken the time to value myself for who I am, apart from the things I'd been used for in my life. I was so willing to give myself away to others in the name of love, of romance, with such an incorrect notion of what that really was. I thought that if I kept cutting out parts of myself, someone would eventually come along and make me whole, but I was wrong. I was finally learning to love myself through my relationship with myself and with God and learning to love others without fear.

Sebastian and I both did Bible studies on our own and together, learning to navigate the future of our relationship while simultaneously working on ourselves. We'd lived such different lifestyles and were now, as Ellen and my friends said, growing up. And I was grateful to be doing so. After waiting for someone to come along and make me whole for so long, I finally learned that only God could make me whole. And with God, Sebastian, and I came together perfectly. So did everything else, not only for this wedding day.

Geoff and his girlfriend were still going strong, and he showed up at our wedding as one of Sebastian's groomsmen with a haircut and a new suit. He'd gained weight, some muscle, too, and I hadn't seen his eyes tinted red in a long time. None of us ever thought we'd see the day that he'd cut his hair, but he did for his baptism, and on the wedding day, he showed up looking as sharp as ever, turning a new leaf. And we all knew it was only a matter of time until he proposed to his girlfriend.

Despite his initial disbelief in my transformation and doubts about this relationship, my Dad courageously overcame his profound fear of flying to attend my wedding, accompanied by my little sister. He'd never flown anywhere before, and he'd done it just to walk me down the aisle. My Mom was there, and despite their hatred for each other, they managed to be in the same room for the entirety of the event and even took a picture together. It's most likely the only picture I'll ever take of them together, and I cherish it.

The church members and our friends had really come together for us. The piano was played beautifully, and a young woman walked in playing her violin down the aisle. My daughter was a flower girl, and my son was the ring bearer. My bridesmaids paired white roses with their red dresses, and Sebastian's groomsmen wore red ties with their black suits. Red rose petals gracefully dotted the aisle as I walked down, my arm linked with my Dad's, the love of my life on the other end of it. Sebastian's grin spread across his face, his eyes glistening with tears that threatened to fall. I knew they were happy tears, and I knew I had the same in my own eyes.

Everyone says that their wedding day is a blur, but it was vivid in my eyes and just as vivid now in my memory. Sebastian's overjoyed face in front of me at the altar, the reception at a clubhouse in Ellen's neighborhood, the delicious food that a group of church members volunteered to cook, the heartfelt speeches from mine and Sebastian's friends. And the week after, we'd spent only two days on our honeymoon in Orlando when I went back to Fort Lauderdale to bring along my whole family for the rest of the week—my Dad, my sister, and my kids. I never loved Sebastian more than that moment, getting along effortlessly with my family and understanding what this meant for us. And for me.

It was everything, everything I ever wanted. Just like the movies.

Happily, Ever After

It feels like I was searching for love, to be loved, my entire life. I was broken by love because I was searching in the wrong people and places. Finally, after all those years of searching, I found it when I found God.

Through my relationship with God, I learned who I was and what my purpose was in life. And to top it all off, God gave me my greatest gifts: the love story I had always dreamed about with my husband, who loves me unconditionally and has been by my side through all the struggles that we have been through together and unwavering. And my three children who are the love of my life, the reason for my existence, and also the ones that have had a difficult life because of my traumas. But God is helping us work through all of this.

Life did not become perfect or free of problems. It still took me a few years after accepting God to fully understand why He allows suffering—but, as this is not a Bible study, I won't get into that right now. What I can tell you is that, although I still have plenty of problems, I am a happy person. God never promised to take us away from the troubles of this world, but He did promise to give us a sword to fight and that He would be right by our side when troubles come.

My past life was a constant wave of emotions. I would think that I was at my happiest while in a club partying with friends, but the next day, I was depressed at home, searching for the next emotional high. Today, I have a constant feeling of satisfaction with life— even when there are lows, I know it will get better tomorrow. I understand the bigger picture now, the reason God created us and where we are going in the future.

Life is no longer as meaningless as it was when I did not believe in God. When I had my personal encounter with Him, I was at my lowest. I had no self-esteem, I accepted relationships with anyone who wanted to be with me, and I was afraid of one day losing my children. My relationship with God rescued me and showed me how much He loved me and how much I was worth in His eyes. He helped me get out of that sad life and fully restored me. And likewise, God also helped me restore my relationship with my mother. Even though she was not able to fight for us when we were children or help me with my kids, probably because of her own traumas, she did try. A mother who intentionally wants to abandon her children does not come back. And she did, after three months. She left because she was fearful for her life. Even after losing the right to have us, she never gave up on us and faithfully visited us every month. I no longer feel abandoned in the way I was led to believe; my mother was a victim of a patriarchal society, a society that would side with the husband, even in cases of abuse. My identity is no longer that of the "girl who was abandoned."

My relationship with my former step-mother, Madonna, was never fully restored. After she separated from my father, we went on different paths in life and have no contact. However, I recognize today that all the abuse and violence she directed towards me were due to the abuse and violence she received. She was a young woman trying to do what she thought was right. Still, even with the best intentions, she broke me more than the supposed abandonment by my mother. But God showed me that I need to forgive her, understand that she did not know what she was doing, and let go of all the resentment to be able to live in peace. And that is what I did.

Just a few weeks after my wedding, I was baptized. My husband decided to wait a little longer for his own baptism, as he still had to do some more studying of his own. Our decision affected our entire friend group. When they saw our changes and how we were not these sad fanatic Christians like they thought we would be, they craved that happiness in their own lives. Through the influence and love of Ellen, Eliza, and many others, slowly but surely, about 20 of our friends got baptized, followed by 6 more weddings after ours. For many, baptism is the end of their journey; for us, it was just the beginning. Many of our friends were deep into alcohol and drugs, and they all changed their lives. Today, they are also leaders in the church, like me. They all moved to different parts of the world to serve, but our friendship and that time in our lives will be with us for the rest of our lives.

For all these reasons, all I want to do with my life now is serve God, help others know Him, and restore their lives as well. If God can turn someone who felt like the modern-day Mary Magdalene into a wife, a mother, and (the most incredible part) a pastor, imagine what He can do with anyone who's willing to give Him a chance. I could never have imagined that one day I would become a pastor. How that happened is a whole other interesting story, but I will have to share it in another book. It's too much for this one.

The movies usually end with, 'And they lived happily ever after. The End.' But in the movie of my life, it ends with 'The Beginning.'

About the Author

PASTOR CRIS CAZARINE'S life took a pivotal turn when she embraced faith in Christ, marking the beginning of a profound transformation. Her journey with God led her to a fulfilling marriage and, after a few years, a compelling call to full-time ministry. This turning point ignited her passion to serve and became the foundation of her life's work.

Currently, as the Young Adult Director for the Carolina Conference, Pastor Cazarine focuses on nurturing the spiritual well-being of young adults. Her pastoral career began in Raleigh, NC, as an associate pastor, where she fostered community growth and spiritual engagement. Her initiative and dedication led to the successful establishment of a young adult church in Apex, NC, showcasing her innovative approach to ministry.

Cris is a devoted wife to Sebastian and a loving mother, cherishing her family life. She holds a Bachelor's Degree from Southern University and a Master's in Divinity from Andrews University. She actively engages in social endeavors, always eager to share the transformative power of faith with others. Pastor Cris Cazarine's life is a testament to service, education, and a deep commitment to positively influencing young adults through faith, affirming her belief that faith is not just a personal journey but a calling to make a meaningful impact.

Printed in the USA
CPSIA information can be obtained
at www.ICGtesting.com
CBHW050626061124
16957CB00007B/633